W9-AVJ-315

St Paul's

CATHEDRAL

Michelle P. Brown

Welcome from the Dean and Chapter

1

St Paul's is the cathedral church of the diocese of London, one of the greatest cities in the world, which it has served for over 1,400 years. It has become a potent symbol of the life of the nation and is also one of the world's most beautiful buildings, designed by Sir Christopher Wren in the late seventeenth century. Each year nearly two million people flock here for services, concerts, debates, educational events, performing arts and installations and sightseeing. All are most welcome.

4

We, the Dean and Chapter, along with our colleagues – the clergy, musicians, staff and volunteers who care for this much-loved cathedral – hope you will enjoy visiting St Paul's, learning more about the role it has played in history and exploring the treasures and countless human stories that it contains. Most of all, though, we hope it will help you on your own journey of discovery, giving you pause to think and to pray, bringing you ever closer to God and his sustaining love and instilling in you greater love and care for the awesome Creation we are all part of.

2

3

For this place has been made holy by centuries of prayer and thanksgiving; its stones have absorbed the hopes, fears, sorrows and joys of generations and stand as an enduring symbol of our communion with those gone before and those still to come. It is a special place of encounter, for 'This is none other than the house of God, this is the gate of heaven' (Genesis 28: 17). Enter, and be welcome.

Facing page Architectural detail – railing in the gallery. 1 Portrait of the Very Reverend Dr John Moses, Dean of St Paul's Cathedral (1996–2006) beside the Tijou Gates, by Jane Bond. 2 Detail from the Tijou Gates depicting St Peter. 3 Gates leading into the sanctuary (sacrarium), designed in the early 18th century by Jean Tijou. 4 St Paul, surmounting the column in the north churchyard. Overleaf Interior of the Cathedral: view to the north-east, from beneath the dome.

'This is none other than the house of God, this is the gate of heaven'

GENESIS 28: 17

S. MATTHEW
S. MARK

OPERA DOMINI

1

A beacon of faith

The Cathedral in the diocese, the city, the nation and the world

St Paul's has been the cathedral church of London since at least 604, when it became a focus for the conversion of what was then Anglo-Saxon England to the Christian faith. Its founder, St Mellitus, based his *cathedra* (episcopal throne) in what had been the foremost town of Roman Britain – Londinium – and made it the centre of a diocese that grew as the faith spread. St Paul, the Apostle to the Gentiles, was an apt choice as protector for a city at the heart of a nation on the edge of the then known world – fulfilling Christ's commission to the Apostles to carry the Gospel (Old English *Godspell*, or 'Good News'), with its message of justice, peace and love, to the farthest corners of the earth. St Paul became the patron saint of London and was joined in the late twelfth century by Thomas Becket, a Londoner by birth and Primate of the Church in England, martyred for refusing to acknowledge the absolute supremacy of worldly power and authority. St Paul's remains the seat of the Bishop of London to this day, at the heart of an active and challenging diocese where people from all around the world, with a rich blend of cultures and beliefs, live, work and play together.

The fortunes of St Paul's have always been intimately linked to its relations with the lively city in which it sits. For centuries Londoners have had a complex relationship with this icon that has so often represented their home and the nation's capital. It has been the public stage upon which kings and queens, mayors and civic dignitaries, leading public figures and prominent clergy have performed the pageant of history and it has been the altar upon which the rejoicings and lamentations of the nation have been placed before God.

There have been several cathedral buildings on the site of St Paul's, whose significance and fortunes have varied across the ages. In the seventh century it represented the reintroduction of Christianity, literacy and the trappings of civilisation to what Bede described as an 'emporium for many nations' in an emerging state that was a successor to Rome. In the thirteenth century it was one of the biggest and most beautiful buildings in Europe, and probably the tallest, its spire making it one of the earliest skyscrapers. In the seventeenth century it symbolised the rebirth of London after the Great Fire and became the first purpose-built Anglican cathedral and finest Baroque building in Britain. During the Blitz of 1940–1941 its dome rose defiantly above the apocalyptic firestorm that engulfed London – and it still appears every night on our TV screens as a backdrop to news reports.

St Paul's Cathedral has been through thick and thin and has three times been burnt to the ground, each time rising phoenix-like from the ashes as a symbol of steadfastness and hope. A carved phoenix rises over the south transept door with the inscription '*Resurgam*', recalling a broken gravestone that was discovered by workmen when the foundations of the current building were laid and which the

The dome and the west façade pediment, with sculptures by Francis Bird (St Paul crowns the apex).

1 St Paul's Cathedral by night. 2 Finial in the form of the British crown and a detail from the glass screen to the OBE Chapel, depicting a Canadian 'mountie'. 3 Detail from the dome mosaics in the quire, depicting the beasts. 4 Detail from the glass screen to the OBE Chapel, depicting a kangaroo (representing Australia). 5 The west façade. 6 The Cathedral viewed from the South Bank of the River Thames.

architect, Sir Christopher Wren, placed as a marker for the centre-point of the dome, for it means 'I shall rise again'.

The building, which still presides over a skyline stretching ever closer to the heavens, is a great masterpiece of Baroque architecture that arose from the pyre of the Great Fire of London (1666). It speaks of the Age of Enlightenment, when the relationships between faith, science and reason were explored, their reconciliation symbolised by the uplifting, unifying dome. This sublime structure was conceived by Wren – a man of faith and a founder of the pioneering scientific Royal Society – using geometric principles; it resembles a giant celestial observatory, uniting humanity and the Divine. Today, as the languages of theology and quantum physics move ever closer, its symbolism of a harmonious, integrated Creation and its exploration of the relationship of the individual to the whole remain vibrant and eloquent.

Yet the story of St Paul's is longer and even more complex than what is represented in the magnificent seventeenth-century building we see today. In exploring its history we unfold the history of the city and the nation. In order to understand how it has evolved and its place within society we need to consider where it has been – and where it is going.

St Paul's is as amazing, as vulnerable and as fallible as the humans who pass through its doors: sometimes sublimely beautiful, sometimes ugly or scarred; sometimes wealthy, sometimes poor; sometimes warm, generous and outgoing, sometimes defensive and self-absorbed. It is sometimes a place of conflict, sometimes a peacemaker; sometimes a pillar of the Establishment, sometimes a radical and prophetic voice; sometimes a bottomless well of the spirit, sometimes arid and thirsting. Its 'feet' are of London clay but, like us, it reaches out with all its might for heaven, seeking fulfilment and union with the universe and its Creator.

1

'We had a mind to build it with a noble cupola, a forme of church-building not as yet known in England, but of wonderfull grace.' JOHN EVELYN, 1666

2

3

4

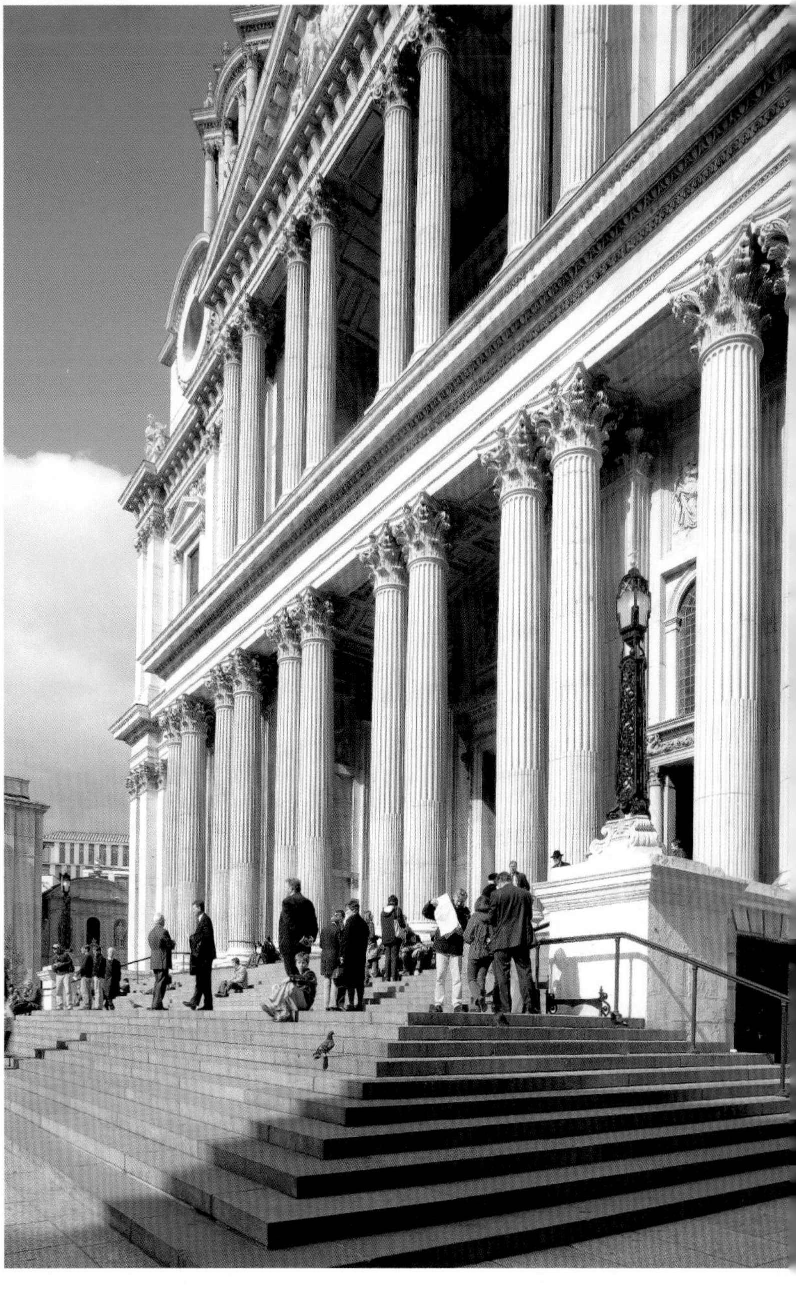
5

6

2

The story of St Paul's

Origins

St Paul's crowns one of two hills within what was the ancient Roman city of Londinium: Ludgate Hill, which forms a ceremonial western approach to St Paul's, recalls the Celtic deity Lugh (King Lud), after whom it may have been named.

Christianity was introduced into Britain as part of the Roman Empire, perhaps as early as the first century. London has always been receptive to new ideas and its earliest named bishop, Augulos, was celebrated as one of the first British martyrs. By the fourth century, when Christianity became the state religion, the Church in Britain had been organised into territorial dioceses – at least four bishoprics existed by the time of the Council of Arles in 314, whose delegates included Bishop Eborius of York and Bishop Restitutus of London.

We do not know where Restitutus was based, but it was probably on the current site that St Mellitus (died 624) founded his cathedral in 604, dedicated to St Paul – Apostle to the Gentiles. This was part of the mission to convert the pagan Germanic settlers (Anglo-Saxons) who carved out kingdoms following the official Roman withdrawal in 410. Mellitus was sent from Rome by Pope Gregory the Great to reinforce this mission, launched by St Augustine in 597 and based in Canterbury because of the support of the Kentish king, Ethelberht, and his Frankish Christian wife, Bertha. The new political landscape determined that Canterbury and York, in the Anglo-Saxon kingdom of Northumbria, would be the sees of England's archbishops, rather than London, as Pope Gregory had planned.

London lay in Essex, which was slow to abandon paganism. Mellitus sought Pope Gregory's advice and was told, nonetheless, that if a place had been a focus of faith for centuries it should not necessarily be destroyed, but embraced as a Christian place of prayer. St Paul's rests on foundations of tolerance, but in 616 Mellitus had to flee for fear of his life in the face of a pagan backlash, since Christianity was a radical social force that threatened to overthrow the social order. It could lead seasoned warriors to embrace pacifism and, if forced into battle, to go armed only with a wooden staff (as in the case of King Sigebert of East Anglia in 635) and could lead kings to free slaves and forgive enemies, at risk of assassination.

The see of London was re-established in the late seventh century by Bishop Erkenwald (675–693) under King Sebbi – who chose to end his days in poverty as a monk and was one of only two rulers to have been buried at St Paul's (the other being King Ethelred *Unrœd*, the 'ill-advised' or 'unready'). This formed part of the organisation of the early English Church by Archbishop Theodore, a learned Greek from Tarsus in Asia Minor. He was assisted by Abbot Hadrian of Canterbury who was born in North Africa – this was a world in which people and ideas travelled. Erkenwald rebuilt the cathedral in stone in 685 and also founded a monastery

The Whispering Gallery beneath the dome, with console decorated with a cherub and the cross-swords, the emblem of St Paul's Cathedral signifying the saint's martyrdom.

1

1 St Peter's Church, Bradwell-on-Sea, Essex, built by St Cedd in Roman fashion, in the mid-seventh century. It may resemble the early cathedral building.
2 Viking gravestone with the lion, symbol of Resurrection and kingship of early eleventh-century date; excavated from the south churchyard of St Paul's in 1852. (Museum of London).
3 The lapidarium, south triforium.

2

3

at Chertsey and a nunnery at Barking for his sister, Abbess Ethelburga. A church dedicated to her in the City of London (Bishopsgate) bore the brunt of a terrorist bombing in 1997 and is now restored as a vibrant centre for reconciliation and peace. St Erkenwald's shrine became a major focus of pilgrimage and healing throughout the Middle Ages, until demolished in 1541 during the Reformation. It was particularly associated with eye disease (and thereby with the scriveners whose job caused short-sightedness) and with the legal profession, owing to a later medieval reworking of Erkenwald's 'life' in which he was said to have baptised a just judge from ancient pagan times who was buried beneath the 'New Work' and who was briefly brought back to life for the purpose in order to redeem his soul.

From the seventh century onwards, gifts of land were made to St Paul's to support its mission, extending its diocesan authority into the environs of the city and into Essex, Middlesex, Hertfordshire and Wessex. Some formed the basis of the medieval prebendaries, and the priests who hold them still participate in cathedral life and services today. St Paul's owns little property now, but retains one of its most ancient estates – Tillingham on the Essex coast. Adjacent to it stands a precious church – St Peter's at Bradwell-on-Sea, set in the ruined Roman fort of Othona – built in the mid-seventh century by St Cedd, a missionary from Lindisfarne in Northumbria who helped to reconvert Essex. This may resemble the early church of St Paul's, particularly that reconstructed in stone by Erkenwald in 685. Most of these details are recounted by the Northumbrian monk Bede (died 735) in his *Ecclesiastical History of the English People*, some research for which was conducted by the first named priest of the London diocese, Nothelm, at the papal archives in Rome.

St Paul's fortunes fluctuated with London's as various kingdoms competed for ownership of this important trading centre, until Viking raiders seized control during the ninth century. In 886 King Alfred the Great retook London and reoccupied the royal palace close to St Paul's. It was probably a St Paul's scribe who, between 886–890, drew up Alfred and Guthrum's *Frith*, the treaty by which he and the leader of Viking forces in East Anglia established the boundaries and legal distinctions between free England

TIMELINE

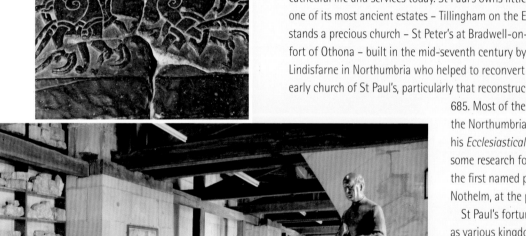

c. 30	43	c. 65	313	314	410	570	597	604
Crucifixion and Resurrection of Christ	Emperor Claudius invades Britain	Death of St Paul	Edict of Milan: Emperor Constantine grants toleration to Christians	**Bishop Restitutus of London attends Council of Arles**	Emperor Honorius recalls Roman troops from Britain	Birth of the Prophet Muhammad	St Augustine's mission from Rome arrives in Canterbury	**St Mellitus founds St Paul's Cathedral**

and the Danelaw, which ensured a measure of stability and safety for all. During the tenth century the Cathedral participated in the Church revival, one of whose masterminds, St Dunstan, served as Bishop of London in 959, and formulated its own influential liturgy (which it developed and determinedly retained until *Sarum Use* was imposed in 1414). But it remained a secular cathedral, retaining canons rather than becoming a reformed Benedictine monastery like most of its peers. In 962 London witnessed the first of a series of devastating fires. The *Anglo-Saxon Chronicle* records that a great pestilence occurred and a fire in London destroyed St Paul's, which was rebuilt that same year. The same series of events would be repeated in 1666 – but Wren's new cathedral took much longer to build.

The pagan Viking threat did not disappear and it was at St Paul's that Bishop Wulfstan (996–1002) began preaching resistance and where the body of Archbishop Alphege, beaten to death at Greenwich by drunken Vikings with bones left over from their feast, was initially buried. The Vikings gradually converted to Christianity and integrated into society, however, and several Anglo-Scandinavian tombstones have been excavated from the Cathedral churchyards.

Also within the Cathedral precinct, in its north-east corner, lay the *folkmoot* or assembly place where, under Anglo-Saxon law, the people gathered to have their say in government. By 1241 its focus had become Paul's Cross, just outside the north-east corner of the Cathedral, where public declarations were made and sermons were preached – contributing to the growth of freedom of speech. The stream of information it provided for Londoners and the world at large continued to flow across the ages, running down Ludgate Hill and into Fleet Street, home of the newspaper industry. The north-east churchyard of St Paul's retained its role as a proto-parliament for the citizens of London and as a place of public assembly, contributing to the development of democracy, until largely supplanted during the fourteenth century by the newly constructed Guildhall. Yet as late as the early seventeenth century thousands of people are reported as gathering to worship, in lively fashion, around Paul's Cross.

Under King Edward the Confessor London gained another religious and governmental focus at Westminster, with its palace and abbey, and increasing Continental influence was introduced. At the time of the Norman Conquest in 1066, the Bishop of London, William, was himself a Norman, as was his predecessor, Robert of Jumièges. This may have helped to ensure that St Paul's lost less land to William the Conqueror's knights and suffered less disruption than most English sees as the feudal age began.

4

4 Possible fragment from the shrine of St Erkenwald (died 693; feast 30 April), Bishop of London, the leading saint whose relics were kept at St Paul's. These were translated several times, including to this, the latest shrine, on 1 February 1326. Located in the lapidarium, a collection of stones from former cathedrals excavated on site (Cathedral Collections).
5 The shrine of St Erkenwald as it appeared from 1326 until despoiled by Henry VIII's commissioners and destroyed in the Great Fire of London, from William Dugdale's *History of St Paul's* (1658).

5

622	638	653	c. 670	685	690	691	751	752	800
The Hejira, the Prophet Muhammad's flight from Mecca	Jerusalem under Muslim rule (until 1099)	Text of the Qur'an codified	Hindu 'Seven 'Pagodas' at Mahabalipuram near Madras built	**St Erkenwald rebuilds St Paul's in stone**	Empress Wu comes to power in China	Dome of the Rock built in Jerusalem	Chinese lose control of Silk Route	Great Buddha of Nara erected in Japan	Emperor Charlemagne crowned in Rome

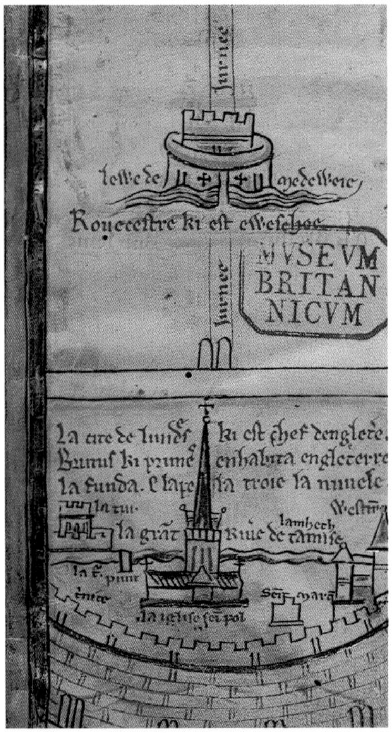

1

2

1 Map depicting the pilgrimage route from London to Apulia, by the St Albans monk and chronicler, Matthew Paris, prefacing his *History of the English* of c.1252. London, dominated by St Paul's Cathedral, appears at the bottom (British Library, Royal MS 14.C.vii. f.2r).
2 The quire of St Paul's in the thirteenth century, from William Dugdale's *History of St Paul's* (1658).

The Medieval Cathedral

In 1087 St Paul's was once more burnt to the ground by a fire that swept through London. The replacement that Bishop Maurice (1085–1107) began constructing was one of the largest structures built in Europe since the Romans. Norman kings and bishops recognised its importance as a public space and focus of faith within their wealthiest city, which was becoming the seat of national power and royal authority. From around 1200 the City's square mile became virtually a state within a state – and at times even envisioned a future as a commune, independent of the rest of the nation. Traditionally, it governed much of its own affairs and the monarch is still given the Lord Mayor's symbolic permission to enter it by the handing over of the sword of state (by which he governs the City on behalf of the Crown).

The area around St Paul's became a defensive bastion at the western end of the City, complementing the Tower of London to the east, a feature recalled by the nearby 'Old Bailey' and designed to control as well as to protect the populace. By the time of Bishop Maurice the role of dean had appeared, becoming leader of the Chapter of Canons running the Cathedral under Dean Ralph de Diceto in the late twelfth century. One of his junior canons was Thomas Becket, born in nearby Cheapside, to whom the chapel in St Paul's Deanery was dedicated, following his martyrdom by Henry II's knights when he was Archbishop of Canterbury. The canons formed the household (*familia*) of the bishop, but from this period Chapter also evolved a relatively independent identity, with a financial endowment distinct from that of the bishop, a remit to maintain the worship of the Cathedral, and a role in furthering its wider mission, led by the bishop. This collaboration continues today.

The medieval cathedral was begun around 1087 and in 1148 St Erkenwald's relics were translated to its high altar where they became the central cult focus, along with those of St Mellitus. Other popular relics included the jawbone of King Ethelberht of Kent and the staff of Thomas Becket. By 1175 the Cathedral was largely complete, although its tower and spire were not finished until 1221. The building was dedicated in 1240 but work did not end there; its east end was extended in the 'New Work' – a large quire to accommodate the growing body of clergy and choir, a lady chapel, the shrine of St Erkenwald and other monuments. This was completed in the 1320s, and a new chapter house and cloister were added by royal mason William Ramsay in 1332. Other buildings sprang up around the precinct during the fourteenth and fifteenth centuries, including a college for the Minor Canons (who became incorporated in 1394), housing some 300 cathedral folk.

Inside the Cathedral altars and cult sites proliferated: chantry chapels (up to 74 of them recorded in 1370) where prayers for clerical and lay patrons were chanted;

886	959	962	1041	1066	1087	1127	1148	1175	1170
Alfred the Great retakes London from the Vikings	St Dunstan is Bishop of London	**St Paul's rebuilt after fire**	**St Paul's Cross has become a focus for public assembly and free speech**	**The Norman Conquest. St Paul's escapes disruption under Norman bishop, William**	**St Paul's destroyed by fire and rebuilding commenced**	**First mention of the cathedral choir**	**Shrine of St Erkenwald moved to the High Altar**	**Rebuilding of body of cathedral completed**	**Archbishop Thomas Becket, former canon of St Paul's, martyred**

monuments to prominent figures, such as John of Gaunt and the saintly thirteenth-century Bishop Roger Niger; images (such as St Uncumber's statue), shrines, chapels and other pilgrimage sites. Amongst the most popular chapels were those of Our Lady in the south quire aisle, St John the Baptist in the crypt below and St Radegunde. Above the north transept door was the famous Rood (Crucifixion), said to have been found in the Thames around the year 140 by the mythical King Lucius, or to have been washed up at St Paul's Wharf, having originally been erected at Caerleon in Wales by Joseph of Arimathea, who buried Christ. Above the south transept door stood an image of the Annunciation to the Virgin. Famous medieval families such as the Luttrells and the Pastons, remembered through their books or letters, visited these images to pray for husbands or heirs.

Fraternities met and worshipped in particular parts of the building, notably the Fraternity of the Holy Name ('IHS', the abbreviated form of the name *Ihesus*/'Jesus', also known as the Fraternity of Jesus). In the crypt St Faith's Chapel formed a church within a church, perhaps on the original site of St Erkenwald's shrine, serving the parish of St Faith's until 1551.

By the time it was completed the medieval cathedral was massive – considerably larger than the present building – and its spire was perhaps the highest in Europe, at a towering 149 metres, making this medieval skyscraper the tallest building to be erected in London until 1964. It dominated London's skyline until felled by lightning in 1561.

As Westminster Abbey developed as the place of royal coronation and burial, while remaining essentially a monastery, St Paul's became England's more public focus for civic and other major ceremonies, affairs of state and public rejoicing, mourning and debate. Monarchs and visiting dignitaries would enter or leave London by processing to or from the Cathedral and would celebrate rites of passage there. Prince Arthur and Katherine of Aragon, for example, were married there with great pomp in 1501 and Richard the Lionheart processed there on his return from captivity during the Crusades. The great processions at feasts such as Whit Week attracted tens of thousands of Londoners, accompanied by the mayor, sheriffs and aldermen – giving rise to a civic liturgy still perpetuated in the guild services and Lord Mayor's Show.

During periods of instability in the reigns of King John and Henry III, St Paul's became a focus for opposition and protest, contributing to the creation of Magna Carta in 1215 – a foundation stone of civil liberties that included provision for the right to fair trial and prohibited arbitrary taxation. On the eve of civil war in 1263, King Henry III held a parliament in St Paul's and when another threatened in 1297–8 it was to the Cathedral that King Edward I summoned a muster of the whole kingdom. Likewise, the great councils of the southern province of the Church in England frequently met at St Paul's, rather than Canterbury.

3

4

3 St Paul's depicted in an early fourteenth-century manuscript about the foundation of London (British Library, Cotton MS Nero D.II, F.18). 4 Funerary effigy of John Donne, poet and Dean (died 1631). Donne modelled for a painting upon which Nicholas Stone based this sculpture, in the south quire (Dean's) aisle.

1215	1221	1240	c. 1320	1343	1381	1406	1455	1505–19	1519
Magna Carta – a foundation stone of civil liberties – issued by King John	**St Paul's tower and spire built, the tallest building in London until 1964**	**Medieval cathedral is dedicated**	**'New Work' of the quire added**	Geoffrey Chaucer 1343–1400	The Peasants' Revolt marches on London	**Lollard followers of Wycliffe preach and protest at Paul's Cross**	Wars of the Roses 1455–1485	**Dean John Colet introduces humanism to St Paul's and founds St Paul's School**	Death of Leonardo da Vinci

1

1 John Colet (1467–1519), Dean of St Paul's 1505–19, humanist, friend of Erasmus and Sir Thomas More, founder of St Paul's School.
2 Dean John Colet (1504–1519), humanist scholar who established St Paul's School in its modern form, depicted by William Seger in 1585 and inspired by Colet's tomb in the cathedral, from the cover of the St Paul's School Ordinances (Mercers' Company).

2

And so, long before Wren's masterpiece took shape, St Paul's had already assumed its distinctive role in national affairs. It was a symbolic meeting point between central government and the people, and between recognition of the economic basis of power and the aspiration to use it wisely in pursuit of the common good and higher, more spiritual goals.

Life was not always so good for the medieval St Paul's, however. Some clergy were absentees who neglected their duties. They did not always get on and tension sometimes arose between the concerns of the Bishop and those of Dean and Chapter. The Cathedral was often caught up in local and national disputes, witnessing assaults in its precincts and occasional public executions in its churchyards. It did not fall under the patronage of any particular party and the lion's share of Londoners' veneration and donations went instead to parish churches, especially those associated with craft guilds. One of the most energetic of London's medieval bishops, Robert Braybroke, who argued for Londoners with King Richard II at the time of the Peasants' Revolt in 1381, tried to revive the flagging cult of St Erkenwald. He had limited success (although in the late fifteenth century craft fraternities seemed to develop a renewed interest in St Paul's, notably the coopers, armourers, dyers, saddlers and scriveners). Public spaces such as the precincts of St Paul's could attract unwanted activity: vandalism occurred, prostitutes solicited, deals were done and crimes committed. In 1385 Bishop Braybroke threatened to excommunicate those who traded in the Cathedral, played football in it or threatened to break windows by shooting at birds.

Around the Cathedral precincts trades and commerce flourished, reflected in street names such as Old Change (where coinage may have been minted and exchanged since Alfred the Great's time) and Seacoal Lane. Manuscript production and music also flourished here, commencing a traditional association of Paternoster Row and environs with the book trade, music making and *avant garde* thought. Illuminators such as the Rhenish Hermann Scheere and the Dominican John Siferwas, who painted some of the greatest late medieval English manuscripts, gathered here along with the scriveners. Inside was also a hive of secular activity during the later fifteenth and sixteenth centuries, with the exception of the quire and chapels. Lawyers and others touted for trade around the font; warehouses and workshops occupied the crypt; and the nave was a thoroughfare, doss-house and scene of the notorious 'Paul's Walk', when those on the make eyed one another up with a view to doing business of various kinds. The scene must have recalled the traders in the Temple, expelled by Christ.

Although London did not become a university town in the manner of Paris or Oxford, St Paul's grammar and almoner's schools for boys, and its academies specialising in theological studies and law, made it London's intellectual hub. By the early thirteenth century its reputation as a musical centre of excellence and innovation was established with early experiments in polyphony, the growth of its choir and the beginnings of a choir school. Images at St Paul's were renowned, the beauty of the building and its contents earning it the epiphet of 'the English Chartres', and its great eastern rose window was so fine that Chaucer quipped of Absalon in *The Miller's Tale* that he was so vain that he had great Paul's east window 'carven on his shoes'.

St Paul's also developed as an institution. By the thirteenth century the establishment comprised Dean and Chapter, Canons (some of whom were residentiary with their own houses on site and who could be married – generally so before 1130 but infrequently thereafter), Minor Canons, Vicars Choral, Archdeacons, Prebendaries, Virgers and other cathedral lay staff. This structure is still echoed today.

The Rise of Dissent and of Humanism

St Paul's tradition of theological learning was challenged from the late fourteenth century by John Wycliffe and the Lollards, who agitated for Church reform and access for all to the Bible in their own language. They posted their articles on the West Door and in 1406 fiery Lollard preacher William Taylor preached at Paul's Cross. Copies of Tyndale's *English New Testament*, printed in Worms, Germany, in 1526 for export to England, were seized and burned there. This was a far cry from the early times of the Cathedral when Bede spent his final days in 735 translating St John's Gospel into English for all. Paul's Cross, that pioneering focus of free speech, could also be one of repression and promulgation of the 'official line' – symbolised by the covered external gallery that was built in the 1480s to accommodate VIPs in comfort. In 1520 Bishop John Fisher denounced Martin Luther's teachings in a two-hour sermon from Paul's Cross, culminating in the burning of Lutheran books, and posted the papal bull condemning Luther on the great west door – where it soon had anti-papal comments scribbled upon it.

The west door continued as a posting board for heretical tracts and its doorjambs are still adorned with the graffiti of centuries, some doubtless inscribed by the ever ebullient and fractious apprentice boys of London. The names of these would-be vandals were often painstakingly engraved in their very best handwriting, betraying their engagingly contradictory ambitions not only to challenge this symbol of authority but to be enshrined for posterity by association with it – typical of the relationship of Londoners with St Paul's.

Dean John Colet (1505–1519) was the son of a wealthy London family of mercers and a humanist scholar who loaned books from the Cathedral Library to his friend Erasmus. He improved clerical standards and strengthened relations with city institutions by reviving the Fraternity of the Holy Name, in part to help fund his promotion of elaborate polyphonic music at which the choir excelled. He also reformed the Cathedral's grammar school along humanist lines, endowing it with property on the east side of the precinct and transferring responsibility for it from Dean and Chapter to the Mercers' Company – the St Paul's Schools descended from it still hold their annual celebratory service here.

The Reformation and the Rise of Anglicanism

The tide of public opinion and information, evangelical learning and protest that swelled into the Protestant Reformation was flowing fast. King Henry VIII's affair with Anne Boleyn and divorce from his first wife, Katherine of Aragon, sealed his breach with Rome and unleashed the Protestant Reformation in England. In 1534 the clergy of St Paul's signed the Oath of Supremacy, acknowledging the monarch as Defender of the Faith and supreme head of the newly created Church of England, thereby retaining most of their property and ensuring continuity in many aspects of cathedral life. The city and nation, however, were divided and the sixteenth century was dominated by conflicts of conscience between Catholicism and Protestantism.

3

3 Eighteenth-century graffiti painstakingly carved on the jambs of the west portals.

1

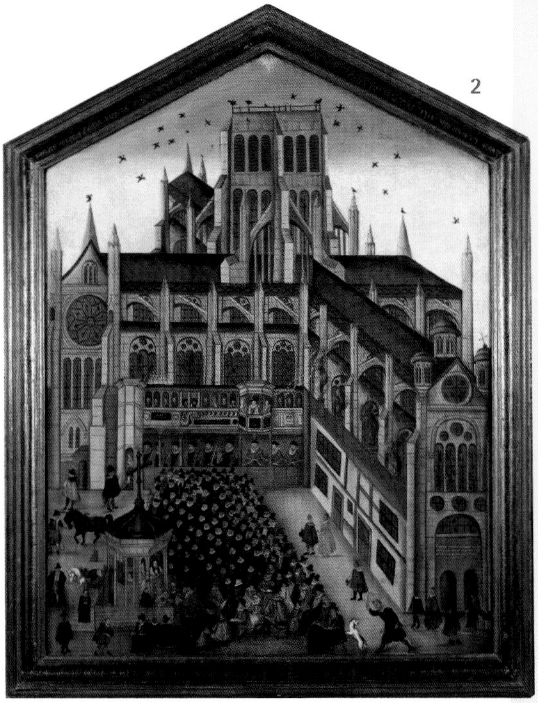

2

St Paul's became an Anglican cathedral, although like others its role was initially ambiguous in the face of the escalating importance of parish churches. Protestantism placed great emphasis upon the Word and St Paul's, with the platform of Paul's Cross and the surrounding warrens of the book trade, remained a focal point. The changing clerical regimes of the sixteenth century, however, regulated the preaching from Paul's Cross, Archbishop Cranmer himself leading a pro-Reformation preaching campaign there in 1536. In response to the Poor Law issued that same year, the Lord Mayor initiated the practice of charitable collections at Paul's Cross – beginning a tradition of charitable giving that continues today. By 1540 copies of the Bible in English were available for public consultation in the Cathedral, inspiring impromptu preaching by ordinary folk. Cranmer's new litany – the first official service in English – was sung at St Paul's in 1545.

Following King Henry's death in 1547 the Lutheran compromises of his reign gave way to an evangelising revolution under his short-lived but staunchly Protestant son, Edward VI, who paused at the Cathedral en route to his coronation at Westminster to watch a high-wire artiste slide down a cable stretched from its steeple to an anchor beside the deanery. This was a rare moment of levity in his brief but action-packed reign. Communion in both kinds was introduced in 1548 under Dean William May, but his removal of the reserved sacrament proved the last straw for Bishop Bonner, provoking a conflict that culminated in the bishop's imprisonment. Many icons and relics were removed, the organ was silenced and in 1550 the high altar was destroyed and replaced with a wooden communion table. And in 1552 St Paul's became one of the first cathedrals to introduce the new Protestant liturgy of the more determinedly evangelical *Book of Common Prayer.*

The situation changed dramatically in 1553 when Edward was succeeded by his elder sister Mary and her consort, King Philip of Spain. They vigorously set about restoring England to Catholicism, and its liturgy was voluntarily reintroduced at St Paul's immediately. Protestant members of Chapter were dismissed, along with Dean May who was replaced by John Feckenham, and Bishop Bonner was restored. Cardinal Pole arrived in England to absolve the nation and reconcile it with the papacy. He was greeted at St Paul's, which became the place of trial of nearly 300 people executed for heresy in 1555–8 – including three of the cathedral clergy: John Rogers, John Cardmaker and John Bradford, Protestant martyrs who joined the ranks of those who had already died for their Catholic faith, fuelling the fires of nearby Smithfield.

Mary's death ceased the carnage and ushered in the reign of Queen Elizabeth I. The daughter of Henry VIII and Anne Boleyn, whom Henry decapitated in his quest

1 Edward VI's procession along Cheapside on 19 February 1547, the day before his coronation, with St Paul's on the right and St Mary-le-Bow on the left by S. H. Grimm, 1788 after a wall-painting in Cowdray House, Sussex. 2 Gipkyn diptych depicting an idealised view of the Gothic cathedral and a sermon being preached at Paul's Cross in the presence of King James I and his family, c.1620.

1520	1526	1534	1545	1546–90	1564	1547	1552	1553
Bishop Fischer denounces Luther's teachings at Paul's Cross	**Tyndale's** ***New Testament*** **burned at Paul's Cross**	**St Paul's clergy sign the Oath of Supremacy**	**Archbishop Cranmer's new liturgy – the first in English – sung at St Paul's**	Building of the new St Peter's, Rome	Death of Michelangelo	King Henry VIII dies and is succeeded by the strongly Protestant regime of Edward VI	**St Paul's becomes one of the first cathedrals to introduce the Anglican** ***Book of Common Prayer***	King Edward VI dies

for a male heir, Elizabeth was a survivor who understood well the dangers of giving opponents no option but to fight. She waited for a year, content with ensuring that reliable Protestants preached at Paul's Cross, whilst allowing the Catholic liturgy to continue inside. But in 1559 Bishop Bonner and Dean Cole were replaced by Bishop Edmund Grindal, an Evangelical newly returned from exile on the Continent, and Dean May. An amended version of the *Book of Common Prayer* (1559) was reintroduced, the altar was again dismantled in favour of the communion table, and surplices supplanted liturgical vestments. Gradually, conservative members of Chapter were replaced with Evangelicals, but as the reign wore on some anti-Calvinist clergy also appeared, notably Lancelot Andrewes.

The political situation remained volatile, with numerous attempts to oust the Protestant Queen, who seldom attended St Paul's herself. In 1570 John Felton nailed the papal bull excommunicating Elizabeth and urging her deposition, to the gates of the bishop's palace and was executed in the churchyard for his pains; and in 1588 the defeat of the Spanish Armada was celebrated at a service of thanksgiving at Paul's Cross. Nonetheless, a *modus vivendi* was achieved that allowed space for personal conscience. St Paul's contributed by helping to demonstrate the opportunities that Cranmer's prayer book offered for promoting the beauty of holiness in the face of puritanical restraint. From the traumas of the sixteenth century was born Anglicanism – a broad Church in which individual conscience could find a place and the evangelical and the liberal 'catholic' could co-exist in fellowship.

Sadly, the behaviour of the Cathedral's visitors did not improve and neither did its state of repair. Tourists climbed the steeple for the view and dropped stones on those below. When lightning struck the spire in 1561 and brought it crashing down, fundraising met with an apathetic response and restoration was abandoned. In the nave the notorious Paul's Walk continued, as described in 1563:

> The south alley for usurye and Poperye, the north for Simony, and the Horse faire in the middest for all kind of bargains, metinges, brawlinges, murthers, conspiracies, and the font for ordinary paimentes of money.

In 1603 Elizabeth was succeeded by James I, son of her executed cousin and rival, Mary Queen of Scots. The tendency towards heightened ceremonial continued at St Paul's, as did its involvement in ongoing religious strife, with four of those responsible for the Gunpowder Plot and John Garnet, the Jesuit Superior in England, being executed in the precinct in 1606. Outdoors preaching continued, boosted by gifted orator Dean John Donne (1621–1631). Donne was an ascetic, courtier and ardent lover; his elopement with his teenage love occasioned his famous epigram: 'John Donne, Anne Donne, un-done'. He was also renowned for

3

3 The west façade of St Paul's with the new portico designed by Inigo Jones, engraved by Hollar for the *History of St Paul's* by the Royalist Sir William Dugdale, who spent the time of the Commonwealth recording England's ecclesiastical heritage, much of which was rapidly being destroyed. 4 Wren's initial designs for the restoration of St Paul's, before the Great Fire, following on from the programme begun by Inigo Jones. The cross-section shows Gothic vaulting on the right and Wren's classical alternative on the left.

4

1553–8	1555–8	1558	1561	1564	1571	1588	1603	1605
Reign of Catholic Queen Mary I and husband Philip of Spain	**Protestants tried for heresy and martyred, including three St Paul's clergy**	Queen Elizabeth I's reign begins	**St Paul's spire felled by lightning**	William Shakespeare 1564–1616	Naval Battle of Lepanto won by Venetian, Spanish and papal alliance, but the war won by the Ottoman Empire	Spanish Armada – sent to depose Elizabeth I and reintroduce Catholicism – defeated	Queen Elizabeth I dies; succeeded by King James I (and VI of Scotland)	The Gunpowder Plot seeks to destroy king and Parliament

1

his poetry, of which perhaps the best-loved quotation comes from *Devotions upon Emergent Occasions, Meditation 17* (1624):

> No man is an island, entire of itself; every man is a piece of the continent, a part of the main. If a clod be washed away by the sea, Europe is the less, as well as if a promontory were, as well as if a manor of thy friend's or of thine own were. Any man's death diminishes me, because I am involved in mankind; and therefore never send to know for whom the bell tolls; it tolls for thee...

In 1500 London had around 50,000 inhabitants; by 1700 this had risen to over half a million, making it the largest city in Europe, poised to become its foremost centre of trade and finance. Its neighbourhoods were taking shape, with distinctions emerging between the commercial City, the gentrified West End and poorer East End. The period was likewise one of tremendous change for St Paul's.

St Paul's had fallen into considerable disrepair and restoration began in 1633 under leading neo-classical architect Inigo Jones, who designed the Banqueting House in Westminster (outside of which King Charles I was decapitated) and the Queen's House at Greenwich, in the style of Italian Renaissance architect Palladio. Jones clad the outer walls of the nave and transepts in a classical skin of Portland stone and added a colonnaded west portico. Funds to restore the 'Queen of cathedrals' were raised in a nationwide appeal led by William Laud, then Bishop of London, who championed Arminian (pro-Catholic) tendencies and ceremonial worship. St Paul's was associated with the Royalist cause - and its fortunes were to fluctuate with it during the imminent Civil War.

2

3

The restoration works failed to halt the decline of the building's fabric or the morals of those who did business there, especially following the execution of King Charles I in 1649 and the establishment of the puritanical republicanism of the Commonwealth. The new government did not favour the Established Church and dismissed the Dean and Chapter (who were later restored along with Charles II). The new portico was converted into shops for seamstresses and the like and the nave became a barracks and stable.

1 Inigo Jones, who began restoring the medieval cathedral in neo-classical style in 1633, from a miniature by Samuel Cooper (private collection). 2 St Paul's, after it had lost its spire, from a panorama of Shakespeare's London by Nicholas Visscher, engraved in Antwerp around 1616. 3 St Paul's ablaze during the Great Fire of London in 1666, by a Dutch eyewitness.

The Restoration and the Great Fire of London

Upon the Restoration of the Monarchy in 1660 King Charles II ejected the traders from St Paul's and returned its quire to a standard appropriate for worship. In 1662 another restoration programme began under a Royal Commission and Wren was invited to submit plans. These were approved in August 1666 but were overtaken by spectacular events.

1621–31	1630–53	1633	1642	1643–1715	1649	1653–1660	1660
John Donne, poet-Dean of St Paul's	Building of the Taj Mahal at Agra	**Restoration of the Cathedral begun by Inigo Jones**	English Civil War begins	Louis XIV, King of France	Beheading of King Charles I; **St Paul's Dean and Chapter abolished; Cathedral used as a barracks**	The Protectorate, under Oliver Cromwell	Restoration of the Monarchy; **King Charles II restores Cathedral for worship and reintroduces Dean and Chapter**

Late on the evening of 2 September in 1666, a year after the trauma of plague had already decimated London, a fire broke out in a baker's shop in nearby Pudding Lane (marked by The Monument). It fed hungrily upon the timber buildings of the City and, despite frantic efforts over four days to extinguish it, engulfed much of old London. Miraculously, very few died, but sadly these included an old woman who could not escape and sought refuge at the walls of St Paul's. She and her beloved Cathedral perished together. Her charred body was seen by sightseers, as was the undecayed body of Bishop Braybroke, which was cast up from the tomb in apocalyptic fashion. Events were graphically related in the eyewitness account of the diarist Samuel Pepys. He was part of a circle of London intelligentsia, encouraged by the scientific and artistic interests of King Charles II, that included the diarist horticulturist John Evelyn and the architect Christopher Wren. Evelyn was one of the royal commissioners charged with surveying the wreckage and wrote in his diary:

> Thus lay in ashes the most venerable Churche, one of the antientest Pieces of early Piety in the Christian World.

King and Mayor quickly set up a new commission to reconstruct the City. Wren seized his chance and, a mere nine days after the fire began, submitted a plan for a completely new urban centre, influenced by modern town planning in Italy and France, with key buildings, piazzas and broad, straight, radiating streets. The eagerness of Londoners to rebuild their homes and businesses and the legal complexities of property tenure and age-old boundaries asserted themselves, however, and Wren's radical vision was never fulfilled. The City remains, to this day, a fascinating warren of lanes and passages, amidst which Wren's City churches raise their elegant towers and spires to the sky upon the foundations of ancient places of worship. Their dedications betray their early origins (such as St Bride's in Fleet Street, named after the early Irish St Bridget), as do the street names: the current Cathedral close, where its clergy and principal officers reside, is Amen Court, in Ave Maria Lane, just off Paternoster Square.

The roof of the massive medieval cathedral had been built of wood rather than vaulted in stone, to reduce its weight, and the fire crackled through it, bringing it crashing to the ground. Attempts to salvage some of the old structure were abandoned as it was unsafe and Wren, as Surveyor to the King's Works, designed a new cathedral at the request of Dean William Sancroft. The old cathedral was demolished with battering rams and Wren eventually incorporated many of its ancient stones into the new fabric – some can still be identified from their carved mouldings, set inside the crypt walls, whilst many more are found whenever excavations occur.

The young Christopher Wren: bust by Edward Pearce, around the time of Wren's knighthood in 1673.

1662–6	1665	1666	1669	1673	1675–1710	1688
Christopher Wren submits plans for the Cathedral's restoration	Plague	**Great Fire of London destroys St Paul's; Wren rapidly submits plans for rebuilding the City of London**	**Wren's first 'Greek cross' design for the new Cathedral rejected**	**Wren's second 'Great Model' design for the new Cathedral rejected**	**Wren's 'warrant design' approved and built, Wren introducing modifications and reinstating some earlier design features**	The Glorious Revolution; King James deposed in favour of William and Mary

Sir Christopher Wren and the Construction of the Present Cathedral

1

2

3

4

At the time of the fire Wren was Professor of Astronomy at Oxford University (for which his architectural designs included the Sheldonian Theatre), with interests in science, mathematics and geometry, in which Isaac Newton considered him to be a leading expert. He was also a man of faith, with a particular interest in ecclesiastical architecture for, as he once said, 'Architecture aims at eternity.' Wise words, given that he was to spend much of the rest of his working life struggling to maintain his vision for his masterpiece in the face of design by committee and perpetual wrangling with royal and ecclesiastical authorities to maintain the cash-flow.

Wren initially designed the Cathedral as a massive dome on top of a Greek cross – resembling edifices erected by the emperors Constantine and Justinian and appropriately echoing its ancient Roman origins. This was rejected in 1669 due to an attachment on the part of cathedral clergy and citizenry to the old cathedral's nave and spire, which had probably been both the largest and most impressive of their day. A second design was produced and, to force his point home, Wren constructed a large-scale model of his dream building, which is now kept in the Cathedral's Trophy Room in the north triforium. This introduced a nave cum ante-chapel but retained Wren's resplendent dome. The patrons were even able to enter the model to view the interior. How could they fail to be impressed? Well, somehow they managed it. They objected to the 'popish' allusions of the dome, with its resemblance to Bramante's planned dome at St Peter's in Rome (and the one executed by Michelangelo), and to Lemercier's for the Sorbonne in Paris; nor did they like its exuberant Baroque architectural repertoire, redolent of the Catholic Counter-Reformation.

Much to Wren's dismay the proposal embodied in the Great Model was rejected in 1673. It must have seemed just as shockingly different and new as the first sleek, modernist glass towers did in the twentieth-century urban landscape. Wren literally went back to the drawing board and produced a blueprint designed to fulfil the clients' expectations – and to show them how misguided they were, for the 'bastard' building that was born of the union of their wishes and those of the architect was a clumsy fusion of neo-Gothic spire and Latin cross plan in a restrained Baroque cladding. Needless to say, this 'warrant design' was greeted with delight by the Church authorities. Charles II saved the day, however, for when granting the warrant approving the work he permitted the insertion of a clause permitting Wren to make any 'ornamental' alterations that might prove necessary and granting him the right to employ craftsmen as he saw fit. The result was the superb structure that we see today, which is a far cry from the officially sanctioned drawings, its happy fusion of the old and the new – the Renaissance dome atop the Gothic Latin cross – embodying the very spirit of Anglicanism.

The Cathedral took thirty-five years to build (1675–1710), spanning the reigns of five monarchs: Charles II, James II, William and Mary and Queen Anne. Construction began with the quire, enabling the first service to be held there on 2 December 1697.

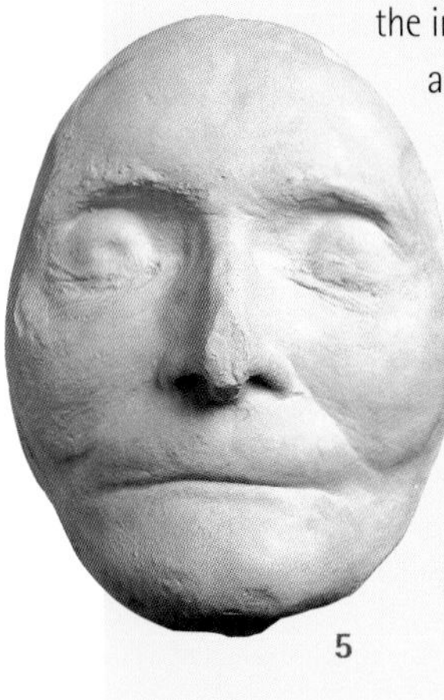
5

1 Wren's 'Greek cross' design. 2 Wren's 'Great Model'. 3 Wren's 'warrant design', from the south side. 4 Wren's pen-knife, with which he sharpened quill pens and erased mistakes when draughting his designs. 5 Wren's death mask, aged 91, on 25 February 1723.

10

6

7

8

6–9 West façade and details of statuary by Francis Bird.
10 The pinnacle of one of the west towers.

9

1

2

3

1 Wren's monument (right) with his son's epitaph to him (top), a memorial to the craftsmen who assisted him (centre) and a piece of Portland stone selected by Wren and bearing his mason's mark (foreground) in the crypt. 2 Wren's definitive design, much as built although many details vary. 3 Sir Christopher Wren as a mature, successful architect, with his masterpiece in the background. 4 Wren's quire, with the organ screening it from the nave, during a service of thanksgiving for the Battle of Ramillies in 1706, engraved by Robert Trevitt. Facing page The west façade.

That same year, Wren's salary was halved to put pressure on him to finish the build. The tenacious pursuit of his vision under such constraints was remarkable. St Paul's finally became the first English cathedral to be completed in the lifetime of its architect – and the first specifically Anglican cathedral to be built.

Tired of interference and hindered by sightseers, Wren clad the building in scaffolding screens, rather like those that shrouded the Cathedral during the recent cleaning programme. By 1709 work was sufficiently advanced to allow tourists access – for an entrance fee, although the building was funded by a special tax on coal entering the Port of London. The final cost was £738,845. 5s. 2½d. – about £50 million today. The first official service following completion in 1710, led by Bishop Henry Compton, was one of thanksgiving for peace following war between England and France. The congregation sat in the quire, along with clergy and choir, and sermons were preached from a pulpit on wheels, moved according to the occasion. As in the Middle Ages, the quire was screened from distracting comings and goings in the nave, but now by the massive edifice of the screen topped by the grand organ (which was set back against the sides of the quire in 1871).

The organ was designed by a leading German craftsman, Father Schmidt, who, to Wren's dismay, insisted on fabricating its pipes on site at great risk of fire. This superb instrument has since been played by many leading musicians, including Handel and Mendelssohn. The impressive wooden carvings of the organ and quire, with its cherubic choirs and floral festoons, are the work of Grinling Gibbons in 1695–9. He also carved the lovely stone floral festoons for the crossing arches. Gibbons was discovered working as a chippy in the dockyards of Deptford by Wren's friend John Evelyn, whose experimental botanical garden – the Elysium Britannicum – lay beside the clamourous docks and slaughterhouses of south-east London.

Wren's vision was realised by a large team of surveyors, draughtsmen (including the young Nicholas Hawksmoor), clerks of works, masons (including the Dane Caius Cibber, Joshua Marshall and the Strongs), craftsmen and labourers (many of whom went on to work on other leading buildings). Wren recruited and supervised the workforce, visiting the site every Saturday, hauled up into the dome in a basket, and regarding it from his home on the riverbank opposite, beside the Globe Theatre. The final stages of the work were traumatic, as the fitting out of the Cathedral and its precinct were taken out of Wren's hands and he had to wrangle with Queen Anne for his remaining fees. Letting go was difficult. Nonetheless, he watched as his son, Christopher, put the last stone in place in 1708 and returned often to contemplate his work, until his death in 1723 at the age of 91. His son composed the Latin epitaph, recorded on a stone plaque above his tomb in the crypt and repeated on the floor beneath the dome.

4

Beneath lies buried the founder of this church and city, Christopher Wren,
who lived more than 90 years, not for himself but for the public good.
Reader, if you seek his monument, look around you.

(EPITAPH BY CHRISTOPHER WREN JNR)

1

2

The Adornment of Wren's Cathedral

Wren had intended that the dome should be adorned with mosaics, like some other great European Baroque buildings, but this was too much for the Ecclesiastical Commissioners who could not countenance such 'popery'. They did, however, accept Thornhill's designs for a scheme of paintings depicting the life of St Paul, executed in a restrained but supremely elegant monochrome grisaille technique, resembling engravings, against a subtly shimmering gold ground. Wren's design for the High Altar was likewise thought to speak too much of Rome, based as it was upon the barley-twist columns and *baldacchino* covering the Tabernacle in the Temple of Jerusalem, which had also inspired that of St Peter's in Rome. It was rejected in favour of a simple wooden altar. This was in turn replaced by a massive Italianate marble altar and reredos adorned with a Crucifixion, prophets and angels, designed in 1888–1891 by G. F. Bodley and Thomas Garner (with matching pulpit by F. C. Penrose). This was damaged by bombing during World War II, and during the reconstruction of the east end in 1958 it was decided to realise Wren's original design for a *baldacchino*, topped by Christ in the act of blessing. The imposing candlesticks on the High Altar are copies of those commissioned by Cardinal Wolsey for his own funeral during the sixteenth century.

The wonderful gates giving lateral access to the sanctuary/sacrarium containing the High Altar were designed in the early eighteenth century by leading French metalworker Jean Tijou, as were the triforium and gallery rails. Tijou also made great chains to help Wren to stabilise the fabric.

Many of the sculptural details and the statuary adorning the building were carved by Francis Bird. They include his exuberant depiction of the conversion of St Paul on the road to Damascus, which enlivens the pediment above the west portico, and the statues of Paul and other saints and prophets who crown the exterior and the imposing font. Other leading sculptors who worked on the Cathedral during the early eighteenth century include Jonathan Maine and William Kempster, whose work graces the library.

1 *Funeral of Arthur Wellesley (1769–1852), Duke of Wellington in St Paul's Cathedral*, engraved by J. Thomson and E. J. Parris. 2 *Funeral procession of the Late Viscount Nelson, from the Admiralty to St Paul's, 9th January 1806*, engraved by Merigot. 3 Cross-section through Wren's cathedral, showing the dome construction and the Thornhill paintings, engraved by Samuel Wale and John Gwynn (1755). 4 Queen Victoria celebrating her Diamond Jubilee at an open-air service at St Paul's in 1897.

3
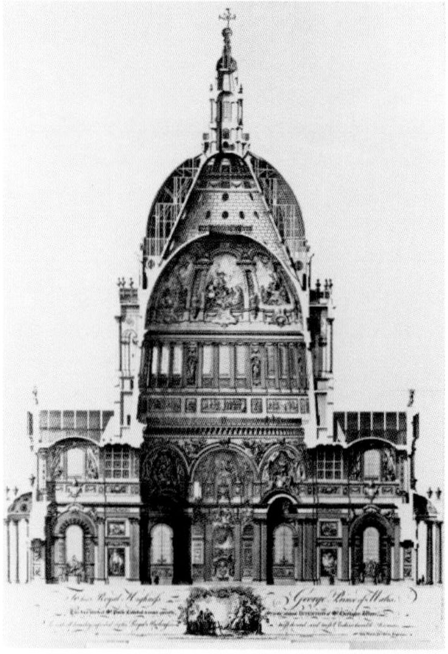

4

The Cathedral from the Late Seventeenth Century to the Victorian Period

As Britain's commercial empire and its territories expanded, so the symbolic role of the Cathedral grew, leading to its description as 'the parish church of the Empire'. The people and their leaders gathered here to seek the Lord's protection, or to give thanks for peace during the many conflicts of the period – the Counter-Reformation struggles surrounding the 'Glorious Revolution', the deposition of King James II and the Jacobite Rebellion, the upheavals of the French Revolution, and the Napoleonic Wars, and the Boer and Crimean Wars.

Particularly grand public occasions included the funerals of Nelson (1806) and Wellington (1852); the thanksgiving services for the recovery from illness of George III (1789) and the Prince of Wales (1872); and the Diamond Jubilee of Queen Victoria (1897), during which the elderly monarch sat in her carriage before the west steps during an open-air service.

5

6

7

5 The north-western bays of the nave, with Wellington's memorial. 6 Architectural detail: pilaster and capital with cornice. 7 Cherubs above the aisle arches.

1 Cherub with episcopal mitre, by Grinling Gibbons, in the quire. 2 Ledger stone commemorating Bishop Mandell Creighton (St Faith's chapel, the crypt). 3 Maria Hackett, who in later life, campaigned tirelessly for the welfare of choristers.

Appointments of Dean and Chapter reflected the choices of the political leaders of the day and were characterised by deans with notable, scholarly credentials – including Hare, Butler, Secker, Newton, Pretyman, Van Mildert, Copleston, Milman, Mansel and Church. The eighteenth-century deans were generally pluralists who simultaneously held bishoprics – usually the poorer ones (Bristol, Llandaff and Oxford), with their revenues from St Paul's helping to support their dioceses (although St Paul's itself only came midway up the league table of cathedral revenues). Although the characteristic defence of Anglican orthodoxy and liberalism was retained, and Evangelicals were often among the leading cathedral clergy, the nature of worship at St Paul's became increasingly ceremonial during the nineteenth century. Several of its clergy were associated with the Oxford Movement, favouring freedom of Catholic worship, which was quite radical at the time. And as the impetus towards political and social reform grew throughout the nineteenth and twentieth centuries, so the clergy of St Paul's grappled with the competing demands of their responsibilities towards maintaining the cathedral fabric and leading a wider Christian mission at the heart of a reinvigorated diocese.

Calls for Church reform and diversion of cathedral revenues to support pastoral work at parish level escalated from the 1830s. Amongst reformers at St Paul's were Sydney Smith (who supported the Reform Bill of 1832) and William Hale. In 1817 Maria Hackett had begun her life's work of campaigning to improve the education and welfare of cathedral choristers – beginning with St Paul's – and in 1845 Hale finally achieved provision for better teaching and housing of the choristers. Preaching was boosted by gifted orators such as Henry Melvill and Henry Parry Liddon, whilst other members of the cathedral complement included William Parker, Secretary of the SPCK (Society for the Promotion of Christian Knowledge) and Minor Canon Richard Barham, author of the best-selling *Ingoldsby Legends.*

Tourism had always been a major factor and in 1837 debate concerning free public access began; the 2d. entrance charge to view parts of the building was temporarily abolished, but had to be reinstated as finances dwindled and maintenance costs escalated. Under Dean Henry Hart Milman (appointed in 1849) and Surveyor to the Fabric F. C. Penrose, there was a movement towards liturgical and devotional innovation, with the introduction of services under the dome (1858) and the relocation of the organ to open up the vista into the quire. They also alleviated the interior's austerity by introducing more surface decoration and imagery.

These trends continued under deans Church and Gregory. The setting for worship was gradually enhanced with glittering mosaics, an Italianate marble High Altar and pulpit and stained glass (designed by the German Nazarene Julius Schnorr von Carolsfeld in 1862 but destroyed in World War II). Practical innovations included the south-west tower clock added in 1893 and electric lighting, paid for by the New

1692	1697	1700	1708	1709	1710	1714	1723	1745	1776	1789
The Salem Witch Trials in North America	**The first service is held in the new St Paul's quire**	London is the largest city in Europe	**Wren's son, Christopher, sets the last stone in place**	**Tourists admitted to the new Cathedral**	**Bishop Compton leads service celebrating the end of the war with France and completion of the Cathedral**	Ascension of George I (beginning of Hanoverian monarchy)	**Death of Sir Christopher Wren, aged 91**	Scottish Rebellion under 'Bonnie Prince Charlie'	American Declaration of Independence	French Revolution begins

York financier J. Pierpont Morgan in 1902. Along with enhanced musical provision, these changes contributed to conflicts concerning ritualism during the 1870s and 1880s. At an Easter service in 1853 a protester rushed the altar, crying 'Protestants to the rescue', only to have Canon Gregory's handkerchief stuffed into his mouth. Nonetheless, congregations expanded as ordinary Londoners and visitors flocked to the Cathedral, with afternoon services in the nave in the 1870s attracting 6,000 people.

The Modern Cathedral

As festivals, charitable services and affairs of state escalated at St Paul's, so too did protests against the Establishment. In 1905 unemployed workers marched on the Cathedral singing the *Marseillaise* and in 1913 suffragettes planted a bomb under the bishop's throne. Cathedral clergy also showed signs of Christian political and social activism, with Henry Scott Holland helping to found the Christian Social Union from Amen Court and working closely with his Tory colleague on Chapter, William Newbolt, in ministering to the workers of London. Together they founded educational initiatives such as a club and reading room, the St Paul's Lecture Society and the Amen Court Guild.

There was something of a setback under William Ralph Inge (the 'gloomy dean', 1911–1934), who described his relationship with his Chapter colleagues as 'a mouse watched by four cats'. The fabric was once again in need of repair and in 1930 the cathedral authorities were served with a 'dangerous structure' notice. Fundraising and works campaigns followed and in 1935 the City of London (St Paul's Cathedral Preservation) Act was passed, protecting the building from environmental disturbances. This upturn coincided with the service celebrating the Silver Jubilee of King George V and Queen Mary (1935).

Notwithstanding, the Cathedral held numerous memorial services throughout World War I (1914–1918) in increasingly democratic vein, commemorating ordinary men and women as well as their leaders. In 1915 Canon Alexander and Surveyor Mervyn Macartney established the St Paul's Watch, a group of over 250 architects, professionals and cathedral staff, which came to include Poet Laureate John Betjeman and art historian Francis Wormald, who protected the Cathedral from fire during both world wars.

The more popular Dean Walter Matthews (1934–1967) included some radical canons in his Chapter – Dick Sheppard and John Collins, who worked to overcome the reputation of St Paul's as a bastion of the Establishment and to make it a focus for Christian social activism and modern music and art. Sheppard led the Peace Pledge Union and attempted to popularise worship, introducing Christmas trees and the crib, but experienced profound frustration at what he saw as an introverted

4

5

4 Angel supporting a shield bearing the Cathedral's emblem: 'D' for 'decanus' (dean) and crossed swords, symbolising St Paul's martyrdom. 5 Bishop Mandell Creighton (died 1901) by Sir Hamo Thornycroft in the south quire (Dean's) aisle. The opulent vestments proclaim Mandell Creighton's high churchmanship.

1792	1805	1832	1852	1837	1861	1872	1897	1901	1913	1914–18
Napoleonic Wars 1792–1815	**Death of Admiral Lord Nelson at the Battle of Trafalgar; his burial at St Paul's**	**The Reform Bill, supported by some St Paul's clergy**	**Death of the Duke of Wellington; his burial at St Paul's**	Reign of Queen Victoria 1837–1901	American Civil War 1861–5	**Appointment of John Stainer as organist**	**Queen Victoria celebrates her Diamond Jubilee at St Paul's**	Death of Queen Victoria	**Suffragettes plant a bomb under the bishop's throne**	World War I

1

2

3

1 The north transept after bomb damage, 17 April 1941. 2 A member of St Paul's Watch guarding the Cathedral's rooftop during the Blitz. 3 Iconic photograph by Herbert Mason showing St Paul's towering above the conflagration of the Blitz on the night of 29 December 1940. 4 The state funeral of Sir Winston Churchill at St Paul's in 1965.

4

preoccupation with cathedral affairs on the part of colleagues such as the stalwart Canon Alexander. Interesting developments were afoot, but these were difficult, confrontational times – within Chapter as well as in the world at large.

Led by Dean Matthews and Surveyor Godfrey Allen, the St Paul's Watch was formed to save St Paul's during World War II (1939–1945); 28 incendiary bombs fell on it during one night alone: 29 December 1940 – the Blitz. Direct hits damaged the High Altar and the north transept but, miraculously, there was no loss of life at the Cathedral; tragically, however, some 40,000 Londoners lost their lives and the surrounding area was flattened. Sir Winston Churchill had phoned the City authorities on that fateful night to say, 'at all costs St Paul's must be saved', for it had become a symbol of national and international resistance to repression and fascism and represented the survival of beauty and the human spirit in the face of horror and destruction. Important services during these years included a service of thanksgiving for deliverance during the Battle of Britain (1943), a memorial service for President Roosevelt (1945) and a VE Day celebratory service (1945), when some 35,000 people gathered around the Cathedral to rejoice.

Members of the St Paul's Watch established the Friends of St Paul's in 1952, which flourished under the active patronage of the late Queen Mother. The Friends still support the Cathedral and 'Working Friends' provide invaluable assistance with guided tours and other essential tasks. The Cathedral revelled in its post-war popularity and set about mounting the St Paul's Campaign to repair the bomb damage. Canon John Collins founded the Campaign for Nuclear Disarmament (CND) in his Amen Court residence (and was arrested during an anti-nuclear protest in Trafalgar Square in 1962) and applied his Christian Action initiative to the South African anti-apartheid movement. He also opened the pulpit to non-conformists and laity (including Martin Luther King and his widow, Coretta) and was even accused of using the Cathedral to advance Communism. Radical times indeed.

Under Dean Sullivan the emphasis fell on pastoral activities and music. The 1960s also witnessed a festival of youth in the crypt, jazz services, folk-dancing, Mary Hopkin singing beneath the dome and the Catholic Cardinal Heenan preaching from the pulpit. In 1977 a service celebrated the Queen's Silver Jubilee. (The splendid vestments worn by the Bishop, Gerald Ellison, embroidered by Beryl Dean with images of St Paul's and London churches, are still displayed and sometimes worn.)

The next dean, Alan Webster, was a theological liberal who, with his wife Margaret, advocated ordination of women and promoted the Cathedral as a focus for urban renewal and dialogue between the wealthy City and the disadvantaged – at the height of the Thatcherite regime. In 1981 the Cathedral staged the spectacular wedding of Prince Charles and Lady Diana Spencer and in 1982 Dean

1915	1935	1939–45	1940	1943	1945	1946	1952
St Paul's Watch formed to protect the Cathedral from fire during war	**King George V and Queen Mary celebrate their Silver Jubilee at St Paul's**	World War II	**The Blitz; 28 bombs landed on St Paul's; it survived thanks to St Paul's Watch**	**Service of Thanksgiving for deliverance during the Battle of Britain**	**VE Day service, celebrating the end of war** Atom bombs dropped on Hiroshima and Nagasaki	**VJ Day service held celebrating the end of the war with Japan**	Ascension of Queen Elizabeth II; The Friends of St Paul's founded, under the patronage of the late Queen Mother

and Chapter incurred Mrs Thatcher's wrath for refusing to celebrate the Falklands War as a victory, preferring a service of remembrance. In 1986–7 the Taizé community held services in the Cathedral, the seating removed to accommodate 7,000 worshippers, standing or kneeling in medieval fashion. Tourism was on the rise and during the 1980s new facilities were put in place to enhance the visitors' experience. In 1990 the Care of Cathedrals Measure provided for cathedrals to establish Fabric Advisory Committees composed of professionals who, under the supervision of the Cathedrals Fabric Commission for England, advise Chapter on such matters – one of many positive collaborations with broader Church and lay communities.

Dean Webster was succeeded by Eric Evans, who made a significant contribution despite, sadly, being afflicted by ill health and died in post in 1996, to be succeeded by Dean John Moses, former provost of Chelmsford Cathedral. Under his inspiring leadership a massive programme for the restoration and cleaning of the interior and exterior of the Cathedral has been successfully undertaken, with funds raised by the Cathedral Foundation. The innovative St Paul's Institute was established (2002) to promote ethical debate, the Cathedrals Measure of 1999 was implemented, and the constitution and statutes revised. In accordance with this, a council was convened to support the work of the Cathedral and three lay members of Chapter were appointed to enhance its skills base.

The first of these voluntary Lay Canons (appointed in 2000) was Peter Chapman, a former chorister and City accountant belonging to the FSA (Financial Services Agency). The second, Claire Foster, adviser to the Church of England on ethics, medicine and the environment, became the first female member of Chapter (2002). The third (2004), Professor Michelle Brown, is an author, historian and curator of materials associated with Christian heritage. They formed part of a diverse but truly collaborative team, along with the ordained, residentiary members of Chapter as it was then constituted: Canon Philip Buckler, the Treasurer; Canon Edmund Newell, the Chancellor and Director of the St Paul's Institute, with a background in economics; Canon Martin Warner, the Canon Pastor and a former Administrator of the Anglican shrine of Walsingham; and Canon Lucy Winkett, the Precentor – whose arrival as a Minor Canon in 1997 marked the introduction of female clergy to the Cathedral and who, in 2003, became the first ordained woman on its Chapter.

5

5 Canon John Collins (second from the right at the front) leading a CND march from Aldermaston, 30 March 1959 6 The wedding of HRH Prince Charles and Lady Diana Spencer, 1981. 7 HM The Queen with Dean and Chapter, 60th Anniversary of the founding of the United Nations. 8 Dean and Chapter, 2006.

6

7

8

1960s	1977	1981	1997	2000	2001	2004	2005
CND founded in the home of Canon Collins of St Paul's; Martin Luther King preaches	Queen Elizabeth II celebrates her Silver Jubilee at St Paul's	Wedding of Prince Charles to Lady Diana Spencer at St Paul's	First woman member of the St Paul's clergy	First Lay Canons admitted to the Chapter of St Paul's	St Paul's Institute founded; memorial service for victims of 9/11 terrorist attack on New York	1,400th anniversary of the Cathedral's foundation	Memorial service for tsunami victims; Make Poverty History campaign – Kofi Annan speaks at St Paul's

1

2

1 Pipework of the great organ.
2 Herbert Howells' autographed manuscript of his *Magnificat and Nunc Dimittis*, composed in 1951 (St Pauls' Cathedral Library). 3 Choristers rehearsing. 4 The diapason chorus, western gallery of the nave.
Facing page Trumpeting angel on the pulpit.

Music at St Paul's

Music is central to the life of the Cathedral and its worship. It is a language that can be understood by people of every nationality and background; it enriches our experience and enlivens the spirit, drawing us closer to God. The gift of music is particularly valuable in a church with congregations formed of locals, visitors from other parts of Britain and around the world, of all ages and from all walks of life. It complements and challenges Wren's majestic building and might in one sense be thought of as fluid architecture, just as the fabric resembles frozen music. The beauty of worship has been significantly enhanced by music and art since the Cathedral's beginnings – and continues to be so today.

The Precentor oversees the liturgical and musical provision at the Cathedral. Services are generally planned by the Minor Canons who, along with the Residentiary Canons, preside over most services. The Organist is also the Director of Music and, along with the Sub-Organist(s) and organ scholar, plays the organ at services and concerts and conducts the choir. The Cathedral choir currently consists of twelve Vicars Choral, six Assistant Vicars Choral and the choristers (around 40 boy choristers and probationer choristers). It is supplemented or replaced, on occasion, by the St Paul's Cathedral Consort (a choir of Vicars Choral and professional sopranos) and by visiting choirs and musicians.

St Paul's has excelled musically since the Middle Ages, with a choir of men and boys first mentioned in 1127. By the early thirteenth century its reputation as a leading innovative musical centre was established with its early experiments in polyphony, the growth of its choir and the beginnings of a choir school in 1263. Following the campaigns of the redoubtable Maria Hackett, the Cathedral's choir school was re-formed and conditions for the education of choristers improved in 1874.

During the sixteenth century Paul's children, also known as the St Paul's urchins, branched out into drama, becoming one of Elizabeth I's favourite troupes. In the eighteenth century, Haydn described the music at St Paul's as the most beautiful sound he had ever heard.

Father Schmidt's magnificent grand organ has filled the Cathedral with its rich tones since the late seventeenth century. It was particularly renowned for its pedals and for the diapason chorus, a set of pipes that carried its sound to the back of the nave, compensating for the nine-second-echo factor. Also at the west end are the royal trumpets, installed for the Royal Jubilee in 1977. Although live trumpeters are used for fanfares at the entrance of royalty,

3

4

'Behold, I stand at the door and knock: if any man hear my voice, and open the door, I will come to him and sup with him, and he with me.' REVELATIONS 3: 20

1

1 *The Light of the World* by the pre-Raphaelite William Holman Hunt. Facing page The south quire (Dean's) aisle, looking east.

the organ trumpets are well-used in recital and at appropriate liturgical moments such as Christmas and Easter. The grand organ has been played by leading visiting musicians, including Handel (whose *Messiah* is still performed in the Cathedral in Advent), Mendelssohn and, more recently, Gillian Weir and resident Directors of Music including John Stainer and Herbert Howells.

The appointment of John Stainer as Organist in 1872 opened a new chapter in the history of the St Paul's choir. The voluntary choir was reorganised (and the services of its recently recruited female members dispensed with) and from 1873 it became central to the Cathedral's new tradition of oratorio performances. Stainer also established new guidelines for the composition of the choir, which persist today.

The choir sang services throughout World War I but was evacuated to Cornwall during World War II. In 1953 Canon John Collins led a choir tour of the USA and Canada, commencing a tradition of prestigious choral tours and recordings. Lavish orchestral 'July masses' were inaugurated by organist Christopher Dearnley in the 1970s and today the extensive repertoire of music performed at St Paul's embraces works by Byrd, Handel, Mozart, Bach, Poulenc, Stainer, Britten, Rutter and Taverner, and compositions by the recent cathedral musicians, including Organist Malcolm Archer and Sub-Organist Huw Williams.

Artworks at St Paul's

The Cathedral continues to be beautified and the Christian message explored and proclaimed by contemporary works of art.

In the nineteenth century the Dean and Chapter of St Paul's, prompted by complaints from Queen Victoria that Wren's Baroque masterpiece was a chilly mausoleum, began introducing artworks to alleviate its austerity. They began commissioning mosaics that encompass high Victorian art, the Pre-Raphaelite movement, the Arts and Crafts movement and Art Nouveau. It is fortunate that plans by Lord Leighton and Alfred Stevens to replace Thornhill's paintings were not realised however; fortunately St Paul's has successfully evolved in response to the needs of successive generations whilst respecting Wren's vision.

The mosaics make a sparkling contribution to the overall effect of the interior and to the uplifting of the spirit, especially now that some of them have been restored to their original splendour. They were designed by four leading British artists: Alfred Stevens, George Frederick Watts, W. E. F. Britten and William Blake Richmond. They help to show how St Paul's has evolved as an organic building, responding to the worship needs and agendas of successive generations whilst respecting the original harmonious vision of Sir Christopher Wren. He in fact considered mosaic decoration in his original plans for the building and interviewed several Italian mosaicists. This would have considerably strengthened the early Christian, Byzantine and pan-European Renaissance and Baroque resonances of this

1 *Mother and Child* by Henry Moore. 2 Detail of a mosaic, quire gallery. Facing page St Paul shipwrecked on Malta, one of the paintings in the dome designed by Sir James Thornhill. Overleaf The interior looking east from the western end of the nave.

1

ultra 'modern' building, but proved too rich for the blood of the Anglican Church Commissioners.

In today's ecumenical environment the aesthetic challenges facing the custodians of St Paul's revolve more around the wish to foster a prayerful sense of worship and an active sense of mission in a building that is also a leading visitor attraction in a popular capital city. Cleaning has revealed the subtle rhythm of Wren's articulation of space and surface and emphasised its organic ornamentation of riotous swags of fruit and veg – the international spoils of the Age of Enlightenment and a celebration of the bounty of Creation.

Other artistic contributions have included Holman Hunt's *Light of the World* and Henry Moore's *Mother and Child*. Recently, St Paul's has hosted the exhibition 'Presence', sponsored by Bible Lands, displaying contemporary Christian art including Bill Viola's powerful video-canvas, *The Messenger*. For a few weeks in 2005 the westernmost bay of the nave was occupied by Rebecca Horn's *Moon Mirror* installation, which represents infinity as a bottomless well of the spirit; its effect of eclipse and its *camera-obscura*-like perspectives echo Wren's fascination with faith and science. The accompanying sound installation, with haunting Moroccan and Sephardic resonances, recall ascetic desert mysticism and the wanderings of the children of Israel. A further contribution has been the recent installation of four paintings by Sergei Chepik, *I am the Way, the Truth and the Life*, in the two facing easternmost bays of the nave. Its *Nativity*, *Public Ministry*, *Crucifixion* and *Resurrection of Christ* tableaux help to convey the narrative of Christ's mission in an age when Biblical themes are no longer widely understood.

2

Chepik was a Soviet dissident, working in its mental institutions, and now paints in Paris. His journey of faith has brought him face to face with suffering and indignity, with the amnesia and self-doubt of the state and the individual, and with the anguish of exile. Such encounters populate these works and invite viewers to identify with them in the present. They provide a new focus for prayer – in private devotions and liturgical contexts – and introduce the reality of suffering, reconciliation and salvation into the reading of the Cathedral, as you move from the life journey of the nave to the sustenance of worship and communion beneath the dome and on to the east end and the eternal celebration and thanksgiving of Creation.

Opportunities for other artworks and installations, long-term or temporary in nature, are being actively pursued with leading artists and the less famous alike. Such works have helped to demonstrate contemporary art's potential contribution to the building, and the value of such locations in stimulating new Christian creativity. Symbolic, abstract, and figurative narrative art can coexist within the same building, serving different purposes and speaking different languages whilst conveying the same messages and evoking complementary contemplative responses.

For one of the great things about St Paul's is that, like its visitors, it has many faces and, in the true spirit of Pentecost, speaks many tongues when sharing the Gospel.

Plan of the cathedral

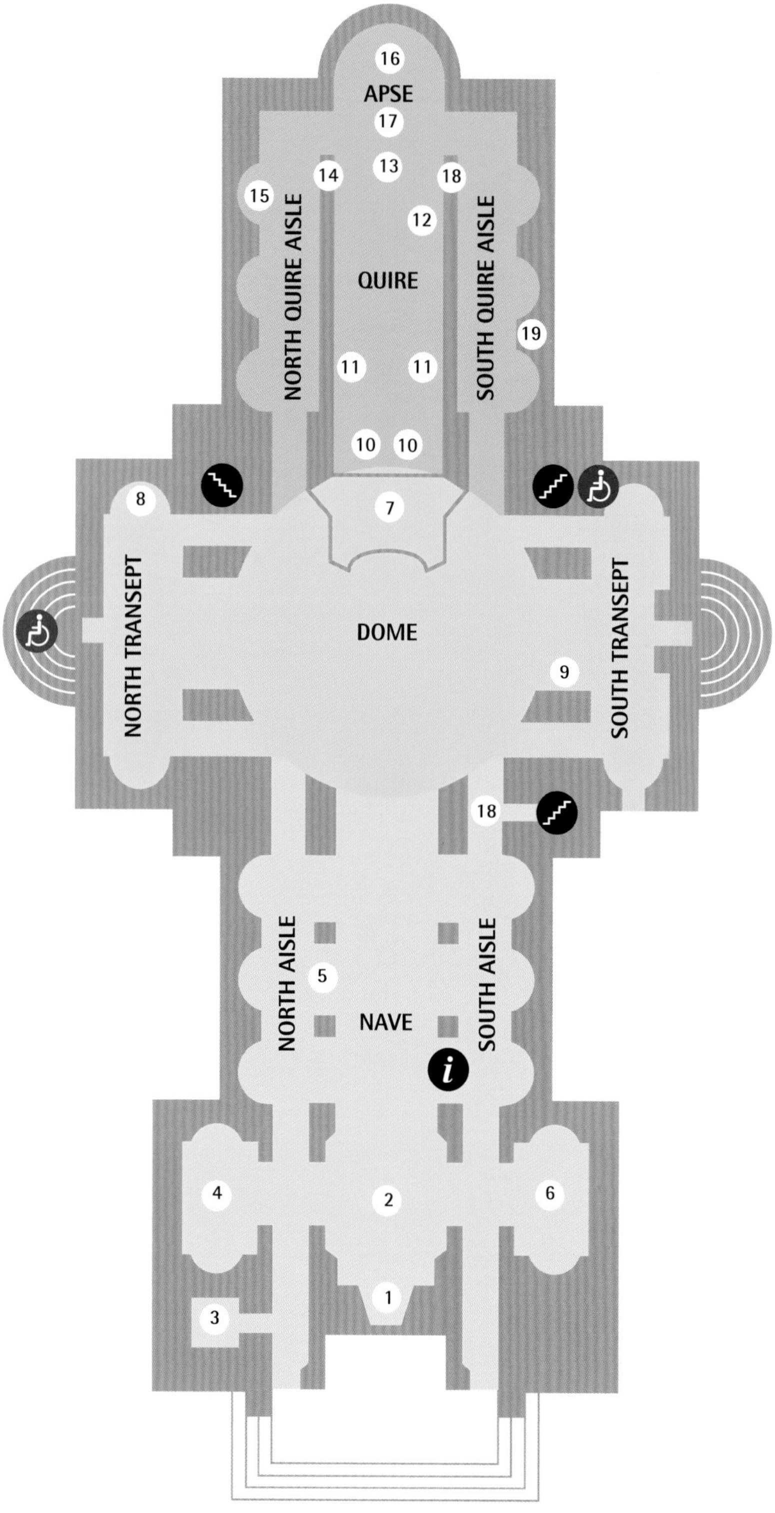

The Cathedral Floor

Nave

1 Great west door
2 Font

North Aisle

3 All Souls Chapel
4 St Dunstan's Chapel
5 Wellington monument

South Aisle

6 Chapel of St Michael and St George

Dome

7 Dome dais with Altar and Pulpit

North Transept

8 *The Light of the World*

South Transept

9 Nelson memorial

Quire

10 Organ
11 Choir stalls
12 Bishop's throne
13 High Altar

North Quire Aisle

14 Tijou Gates
15 Henry Moore's *Mother and Child*

Apse

16 American Memorial Chapel
17 Roll of Honour

South Quire Aisle

18 Tijou Gates
19 Effigy of John Donne

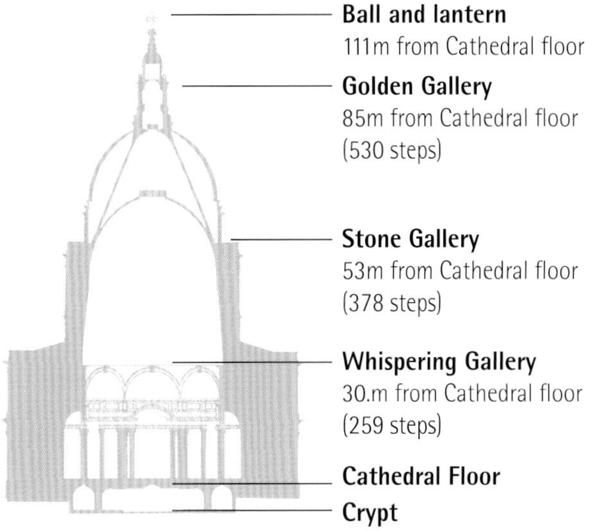

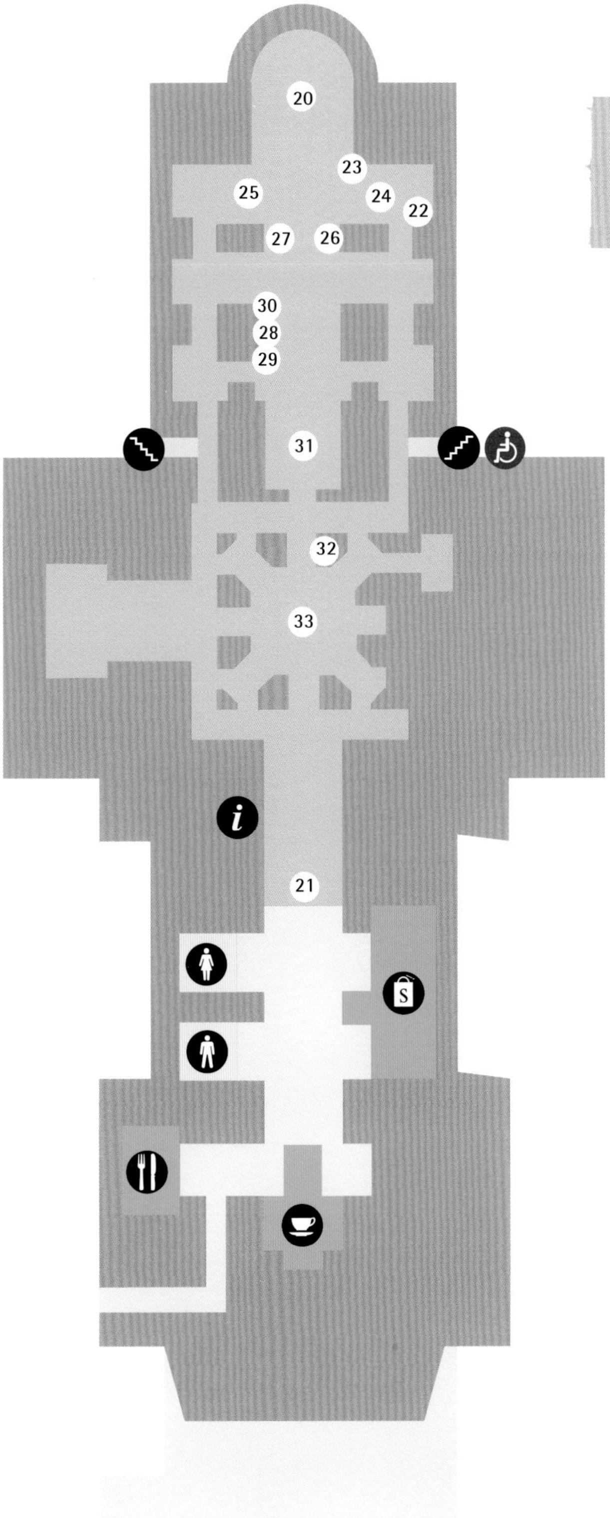

The Crypt

20 OBE Chapel

21 Churchill screen

TOMBS AND MEMORIALS

The architect

22 Christopher Wren

The arts

23 William Blake
24 Joshua Reynolds
25 Arthur Sullivan
26 Sir Edwin Lutyens
27 John Singer Sargent

Scientists

28 Alexander Fleming
29 Gordon Hamilton-Fairley
30 Henry Wellcome

Military and Nursing

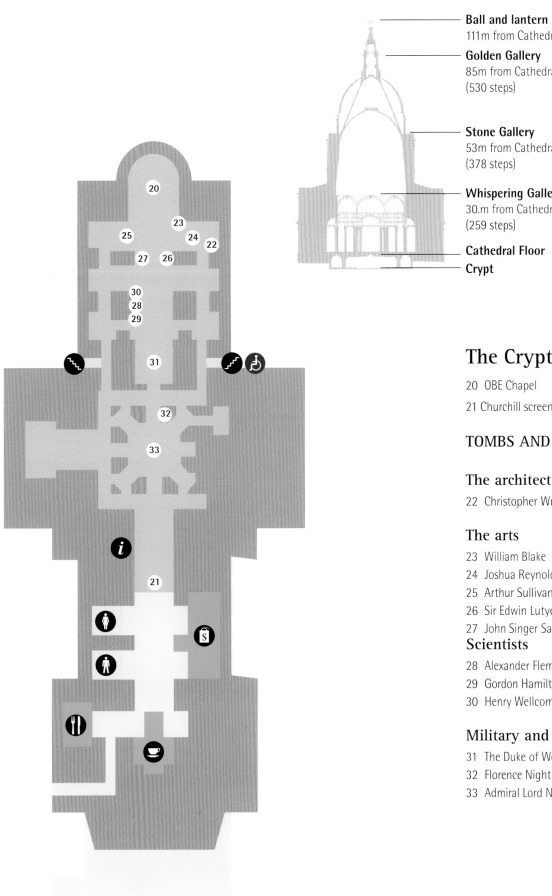

31 The Duke of Wellington
32 Florence Nightingale
33 Admiral Lord Nelson

3

Journey: the **nave** and transepts

The first breathtaking view of the awe-inspiring interior that greets most visitors is from the nave, which leads from the great west door to the dome. It is at this door that Dean and Chapter and the Bishop welcome visiting royalty and the Lord Mayor of London. The public enter through the north-west and south-west doors. On the south side of the south-west tower is another portal known as the Dean's Door because of its proximity to the Old Deanery, built in the 1670s under Edward Woodroffe, which still stands in a lane on this side of the building. Francis Bird carved a tear on the cheek of one of the cherubs above the door, commemorating the death of the dean who commissioned it. The lengthy nave (from the Latin *navis*, ship) was designed to accommodate the spectacle of great liturgical processions when clergy and choir process towards the altar, as they still do each Sunday morning and during special services.

At the western end of the nave stands the font, designed in the early eighteenth century by Francis Bird to resemble a classical urn. Its lid is now kept elsewhere in the Cathedral, to enable easier access to the bowl during baptisms, when new Christians are symbolically washed clean and their lives dedicated to Christ. The nave itself speaks of a journey, of the path that we tread during life and our spiritual journey towards the God who gave us that life.

In the floor is set a memorial to the men and women of the St Paul's Watch who stood guard during World War II, heroically fighting fire before it could take hold. Thanks to them the Cathedral survived the devastating bombings of the Blitz.

Three side chapels stand at the western end of the nave aisles. These are dedicated to Saints Michael and George, All Souls and St Dunstan and are described in Chapter 5.

Wren designed the brass chandeliers in the nave aisles. Those in the nave, which were replaced, are modelled upon those in the near-contemporary church of St Paul's at Deptford in south-east London. The marble floor, with its beautiful black and white geometric patterns, has been heavily restored and altered over the years but was originally designed by William Kempster in the early eighteenth century. The floor vents, with their beautiful brass grilles, served both to ventilate the crypt and to heat the Cathedral above, for fires used to be kept burning beneath them.

The earlier monuments at St Paul's were largely destroyed in the Great Fire of 1666, with the exception of a handful that can be seen in the crypt, the recumbent effigies broken by their falls when the Cathedral's floor collapsed. Some are listed on plaques at the west end of the crypt. Only that of John Donne, from the workshop of Nicholas Stone, survives intact, now set in the south aisle of the quire (the Dean's Aisle), for his snugly shrouded form had no vulnerable limbs to break off. From the late eighteenth century monuments have been erected to commemorate those who have made a particular contribution to the life of the Cathedral or the nation.

Flooring of the nave, with grille encircled by Wren's epitaph, beneath the dome.

1

1 The nave, looking east, around 1725. 2 The font by Francis Bird, and the great west door. 3 Westmacott's memorial to General Sir Ralph Abercromby, who died during the Egyptian campaign in 1801.

St Paul's contains a gallery of some of the finest British sculpture of the Georgian and Victorian ages, featuring work by John Bacon the Elder (the monuments to the prison reformer John Howard, which was the first to be admitted to the new Cathedral in 1790, to Dr Samuel Johnson, of dictionary fame, and to the Orientalist Sir William Jones); John Flaxman (the monuments to Admiral Lord Nelson and Admiral Lord Howe); John Bacon the Younger (monuments to General Sir John Moore and Captain George Duff); Thomas Banks (the monuments to naval captains Richard Rundle Burges and George Blagdon Westcott); Richard Westmacott (the monuments to Lord Collingwood, General Sir Ralph Abercromby and Captain John Cooke); Joseph Boehm (the tomb of General Gordon); and George Richmond (the effigy of Bishop Charles Blomfeld).

An especially evocative piece is *The Gates of Death* in the north aisle of the nave. This is the Melbourne family monument by Carlo Marochetti (after 1853) in which two patient attendant angels guard the gates to the tomb, awaiting the resurrection to new life. The nave is dominated by the imposing marble and bronze memorial to Arthur Wellesley, Lord Wellington (died 1852), who is depicted in bronze lying on its base and on its pinnacle, astride his trusty warhorse, Copenhagen. This Irishman was the victor of the Battle of Waterloo, one of the decisive military engagements of the Napoleonic Wars, and subsequently became Britain's Prime Minister. Designed by Alfred Stevens in 1856, the memorial took 54 years to build (1858–1912) – longer than Wren's cathedral.

The monuments are mostly neo-classical in style and the marble ones they portray solemnly regard the comings and goings on the Cathedral floor, or swoon as they expire in the arms of heroic mythological figures. It can be easy to disregard them, or to consider them anachronistic relics of a bygone, jingoistic age, in danger of turning the body of the church into a Valhalla of martial heroes. And yet, if you pause to gaze at them you will see that they recall real humans and genuine suffering and sacrifice, movingly and aesthetically portrayed.

The monuments extend into the transepts, the two arms of the Latin cross of the Cathedral's ground plan. The monument in the south transept celebrates the life of Nelson, whose missing right arm – lost in action – is cloaked and who is presented as a role model to British children. The nation honoured the great hero, but refused to respect his last wishes that it should support his lover, Emma Hamilton, and their daughter, Horatia, who went to live amongst his French foes. In the north transept is the Middlesex Chapel, described in Chapter 5.

2

3

4

5

6

7

4–5 The Wellington monument by Alfred Stevens, in the nave. 6 *The Public Ministry of Christ* by Sergei Chepik. 7 *The Gates of Death*, the Melbourne family monument by Carlo Marochetti, north aisle of the nave.

4

Encountering the divine

The dome and quire

The Dome

The imposing dome, for which St Paul's is famed, is one of the largest in the world. It consists of a double skin construction, for if its dimensions were the same inside as outside it would resemble a funnel within. The outer dome is constructed of wood and lead with an inner cone of brick, surmounted by a lantern. The inner dome is decorated with exquisite grisaille paintings in monochrome, like engravings, set on a gold ground. They were designed by Sir James Thornhill, who was responsible for the splendid *trompe l'oeil* frescoes and ceiling in the dining hall of the former Naval College at Greenwich, which was also designed by Wren. They depict scenes from the life of St Paul: his conversion, the punishment of the sorcerer Elymas, the Cure at Lystra, the conversion of the gaoler, preaching at Athens, the Ephesians burning books, Paul before Agrippa and the shipwreck on Malta. They were executed in 1716–17 and restored in the 1850s.

Below them are niches into which, in 1892–4, were set statues depicting the Doctors of the Church (or the early Church Fathers who shaped its theology) - Basil, Athanasius, Gregory of Nazianzus and John Chrysostom from the East; and Jerome, Ambrose, Augustine and Gregory the Great from the West. Those who worked in the East now face the western end of the building and those from the West face eastwards, emphasising the ecumenical shared traditions and teaching of the Church throughout the world - for we need each other to be whole.

Beneath lies the famous Whispering Gallery and below this are mosaics depicting Old Testament Prophets (Isaiah, Jeremiah, Ezekiel and Daniel) and the Evangelists (Matthew with his symbol, the man or angel, symbolising the Incarnation of Christ; St Mark with his lion, symbolising the Lion of Judah, kingship and Christ's Resurrection; St Luke with his calf or bull, symbolising the sacrifice of Christ at the Crucifixion; and St John, the visionary, with his eagle who flies directly to the throne of God for inspiration). These were designed in the nineteenth century by Alfred Stevens (the prophets, the first of which was installed in 1864) and George Frederick Watts (Saints Matthew and John) and were completed by W. E. F. Britten in 1888–1893. The mosaics were fabricated by Salviati in Venice.

In the flanking quarter domes are mosaics depicting the Ascension of Christ in which his divinity is revealed; the Crucifixion in which Christ hangs on the Tree of Life, with the waters of life flowing from its base; the Entombment in which the limp body of Christ slumps in the arms of an angel before a sarcophagus; and the Resurrection in which the gates of death are flung wide by Christ. These were designed by William Blake Richmond in 1898-1901 and funded by the livery companies.

The dome rises 111m, or 365ft, like the number of days in a year, reminding us that Wren's building was designed according to geometric and mathematical

St Jerome, one of the statues of the Doctors of the Church beneath the dome; the building and the book signify his contribution to Christian culture.

1 Sir James Thornhill's sketches for the dome scheme. 2 Statue of St John Chrysostom beneath the dome. 3 Detail from Sir James Thornhill's paintings of the life of St Paul. 4 Mosaic by William Blake Richmond depicting the Crucifixion as the Tree of Life. The quarter domes around the central dome. 5 Scenes from the life of St Paul by Sir James Thornhill, the dome. 6–7 Mosaics depicting St John (left) and St Matthew (right) by G. F. Watts, dome spandrels. Overleaf The dome.

principles and symbolic measurements that relate to his interest in astronomy and the relationship between earth and the heavens. This related in turn to his preoccupation with the relationship between God and humanity. He explored this by means of scale and space. His initial designs for the columns of the nave, for example, included massive plinths that dwarfed the humans who scurried between them. The plinths that he built, however, bring the lofty nave down to a more human scale, uplifting rather than intimidating for the worshipper.

The dome is like a massive observatory and symbolises the meeting place of earth and heaven, of humankind and the Divine, united in an endless, encircling union. The spirit soars up into it as you gaze into infinity from the floor below. Around the grille set into it is the epitaph that Wren's son composed for his father (see page 64).

Fittingly, the area beneath the dome – the heart of the building – is now used as the principal place of worship for major services, with a raised dais, wooden altar table, candlesticks and lecterns designed by the current Surveyor to the Fabric, Martin Stancliffe. Beside it stands the pulpit, commissioned by the Friends of St Paul's, from Lord Mottistone, Surveyor to the Fabric, in 1964.

The use of space, music, movement and colour combine to express a unity between earth and heaven that centres on the death and Resurrection of Christ. For this is where people gather in fellowship and, with bread and wine, celebrate the Eucharist in an act of worship that is central to the Christian tradition. This recalls the Last Supper and the body and blood of Jesus Christ, sacrificed for all at his Crucifixion to reconcile and reunite humanity and the world with God. The gold cross on top of the dome symbolises this union and tells the world that this is the mystery of faith held within St Paul's.

1

2

3

4

5

6

7

S. LUKE

The Quire

Beyond the dome stands the quire (or 'choir' as it is often called elsewhere), the traditional focal point for music in worship. Its glittering mosaics and the High Altar beyond impart a sense of culmination and completion and inspire a spirit of rejoicing. This is where, in the Middle Ages, the clergy and choir gathered to celebrate services at the hours of the Divine Office. Since the Reformation and Cranmer's reform of the Office, only Mattins and Evensong feature in the Anglican liturgy. Eucharistic services are now generally celebrated at the altar under the dome to allow congregation, choir and clergy to be more closely united in fellowship (an arrangement initiated in 1858 for Sunday evening services. The morning office of Mattins is said in one of the chapels and Evensong is usually sung in the quire. Thus, during the nineteenth century services moved from the quire because of large congregations drawn by popular preaching; in the twentieth century services used the whole cathedral; and in the twenty-first century choir, congregation and altar have been compacted together in worship.

The dark oak woodwork of the quire stalls and the organ casing was carved with endearing cherubs, trumpeting angels and swags of exuberant foliage by the Anglo-Dutch Grinling Gibbons, master woodcarver of his age. At the south end of the quire is the *cathedra* (throne) of the Bishop of London. Midway along the quire stalls is the 'domestic throne' opposite the Lord Mayor's stall, which also belongs to the Bishop of London. The Archbishop of Canterbury may be lent the domestic throne on occasion. The quire stalls are primarily those of the Prebendaries, but also those of the Archdeacons and the Area and Suffragan Bishops – all of whom make up the College of Canons.

The great organ, designed and manufactured in situ by the German Father Smith, originally screened the quire from the dome. This perpetuated the medieval practice of concealing the quire from the sight of those in the nave and dome crossing – for the quire was the Holy of Holies wherein sat the High Altar, in recollection of the Ark of the Covenant and the Tabernacle in the Temple of Jerusalem. These are also recalled by the *baldacchino* above the High Altar (dedicated to members of the Commonwealth who died in World War II), with its barley-twist columns, modelled on those of the Temple and of St Peter's in Rome, which was erected in 1958.

1 The quire, seen from the dome. 2 Mosaic details from the quire: peacock, symbol of eternal life. 3 Temptation of Eve. 4 Annunciation to the Virgin. 5 The fish of the sea. 6 Adam naming the beasts. Facing page The quire.

2

3

4

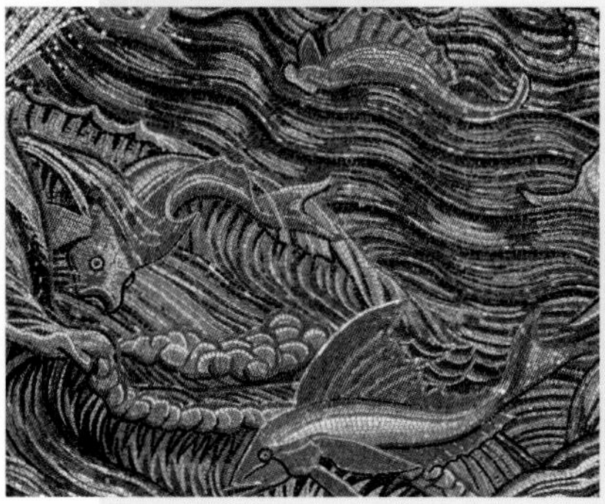

5

6

1

1 Fragments allegedly from the Second Temple, Jerusalem, in the south quire (Dean's) aisle.
2 Stalls in the quire. 3 Details of the mosaics by William Blake Richmond: King David.
4 Christ the King. 5 Birds of the air.
6 Old Testament scene with Judaic menorah.
7 Angel. Facing page The quire, looking towards the High Altar.

It was designed by Stephen Dykes Bower following original designs by Wren that were too extreme for the tastes of his clerical patrons, who opted for a simple wooden communion table, in Protestant fashion (now in St Dunstan's Chapel). For in Wren's cathedral the quire was more the setting of public worship, and less the hidden Holy of Holies, whilst the nave was the setting for secular gathering.

Another reminder of the Temple in Jerusalem are the carved architectural fragments said to come from the second Temple, constructed by Herod, which were brought back from the Holy Land by Canon Henry Parry Liddon, who wrote of his journeys in the nineteenth century. They are mounted on the wall of the south quire aisle. This is also known as the Dean's aisle, for it contains the Dean's vestry, where Dean and Chapter put on the vestments that they wear during services. Sculptures of several former bishops and deans can also be found in this aisle, notably those of Bishop Mandel Creighton (by Sir Hamo Thornycroft) and the poet-Dean John Donne (died 1631) who posed in his shroud for his effigy, which he kept in his bedchamber as a *memento mori* until his death. At the east end of this aisle, at one time, was an altar dedicated to Our Lady, Mary, the mother of Christ.

2

This was matched, in the north quire aisle (also known as the Minor Canons' aisle), by an altar to modern martyrs – Anglicans who died for their faith. In a side bay stands the sculpture *Mother and Child* by renowned sculptor Henry Moore (1984). An atheist, Moore intended this as a homage to the generic relationship, rather than to Mary and the Christ-child specifically. But the celebration of this bitter-sweet bond, and the interlocking organic shapes with their embracing, protective and piercing forms (recalling the prophecy to Mary that a sword would pierce her own heart, and predicting her son's Crucifixion) are particularly apt. Moore was happy for the piece to find its home in the Cathedral.

The wonderful quire mosaics were made in 1896–1904, following cartoons by William Blake Richmond. Those on the saucer domes depict the beasts, fish and birds of Creation, presided over by Christ, the Logos. They are supported by the elegant figures of angels, in Art Nouveau style. On the spandrels of the arcade arches are scenes depicting the Creation of the firmament, the Garden of Eden and Adam and

3

4

5

6

7

OMNES
PECORA
SANCTUS
SANCTUS

1 Columns supporting the baldacchino above the High Altar, based on those of the Temple in Jerusalem and of St Peter's, Rome, twentieth century, after Wren. 2 The High Altar. 3 A prophet depicted on the Tijou Gates. Facing page The cross on the High Altar.

1

2

3

Eve. The inclusion of their naked figures in a place of worship, at the height of the prudish late Victorian era, caused an outcry at the time. Debate was raging between those who subscribed to Darwin's theory of evolution and those who adhered to a literal, Creationist reading of the Bible in which everything was created in six days. It was perhaps appropriate that such a theme should be explored in this great building of the Age of Enlightenment, which celebrates both the mysteries of faith and the scientific means by which they are so often perceived.

Other images in this sequence include King David, the Old Testament 'type' (or precursor) of Christ and the Annunciation to the Virgin, in pre-Raphaelite style, in which is announced the birth of the Saviour who will finally redeem humanity after its fall from grace and its expulsion from Eden. These were joined in 1907 by further mosaics in the quire aisles. Blake Richmond used glass tesserae (set at an angle, in Byzantine fashion, to reflect light) made in London for his mosaics, whereas those in the dome are made from the famed Venetian Murano glass.

The exquisite gilded metalwork of the wrought iron gates that lead from the aisles into the sanctuary containing the High Altar were designed in the early eighteenth century by French master metalworker Jean Tijou. They carry images of the prophets and St Paul with his sword, the instrument of his martyrdom, and St Peter carrying the keys to the gates of heaven.

Behind the High Altar, in the ambulatory, is the American Memorial Chapel (see pages 58–60).

QVAE FACTA SVNT
VIRTVS ET

5 A place for pause: the chapels

It can sometimes be hard to find a place of quiet and solitude in a busy cathedral, but the chapels offer a place apart for reflection, prayer and smaller services. Three side chapels stand at the western end of the nave, off the aisles. That on the south side is dedicated to Saints Michael and George (depicted by Edwin Russell behind the altar) in whose name one of Great Britain's Orders of Chivalry was founded in 1818 to honour those distinguished overseas or in foreign affairs. Plaques commemorating former members of the Order are set on the book rests, and banners of current knights hang above. The fittings are by Mervyn Macartney. It was formerly the site of the consistory court where the bishop sat in judgement over his clergy and later the baptistry.

On the north side of the nave, just inside the door, is the Chapel of All Souls. This contains the marble tomb by William Reid Dick of Lord Kitchener (1850–1916), who reformed the British army, and commemorates those who died in World War I. Next to it is St Dunstan's Chapel, which is set aside for prayer. Formerly the Morning Prayer Chapel, it was dedicated in 1905 to the great tenth-century reforming Archbishop of Canterbury who was also Bishop of London in 959. Dunstan was renowned as an artist – a sculptor, illuminator, scribe and metalworker. His chapel is decorated with nineteenth-century mosaics depicting the women greeted by an angel at the empty tomb, from which Christ arose on Easter Sunday (by Salviati, 1874), and Christ enthroned between the Virgin and St John (by Powells, 1884). Above the altar, which is Wren's original carved by William Samwell, hangs a silver pyx in which the Blessed Sacrament is reserved, designed by Rod Kelly for the Millennium.

In the north transept stands the Middlesex Chapel, dedicated to members of the Middlesex Regiment whose colours hang from the walls. On the north-east side is an altar behind which stands William Holman Hunt's *Light of the World*. This icon of Pre-Raphaelite painting is the artist's third version of the subject, commissioned and presented by philanthropist and shipowner Charles Booth. It depicts Christ holding a lantern pierced by designs of crosses and crescents (indicating that he came for all – Christians and those of other faiths), who knocks patiently at an overgrown door in the woods. The plants that have grown over this entrance, and the absence of a door handle, show that it has remained closed for some time and can only be opened from within. It symbolises the human heart, which Christ is waiting to enter and enlighten, should we but listen and open ourselves to receive Him. This is one of the few paintings that returned to the Cathedral after its treasures were evacuated during World War II.

At the east end behind the High Altar, where the medieval Lady Chapel once stood, is the American Memorial Chapel. This part of the building was destroyed during the Blitz and when it was rebuilt in the 1950s it was decided to form

Lighting votive candles as a symbol of living prayer, St Dunstan's Chapel.

1

2

3

1 Detail from the American Roll of Honour. 2–3 The Chapel of Saints Michael and George, and detail of the Crucifix. 4 St Dunstan's Chapel.

a chapel, funded by the British people, to commemorate the members of the United States forces based in Britain who gave their lives defending liberty during World War II. In a case behind the High Altar (itself dedicated to members of the Commonwealth who died in that same war) is an illuminated book of remembrance – the American Roll of Honour presented by General Eisenhower in 1951 – in which their 28,000 names are inscribed. The American Chapel was designed by Stephen Dykes Bower and constructed by Godfrey Allen, Surveyor to the Fabric, and the images that adorn its wood, metalwork and stained glass include depictions of the flora and fauna of North America and references to historical events such as the foundation of the English settlement of Jamestown (Virginia) in 1607, the signing of the Declaration of Independence in 1776 and space exploration signified by a carved rocket. References to Moses commemorate the many Jews who fought in the war. Many US citizens, including the families of those commemorated, come here to pray and to remember.

In the crypt are the Chapel of St Faith, OBE Chapel and the Chapel of the Imperial Society of Knights Bachelor. There has been a chapel dedicated to St Faith here since the Middle Ages, when building works necessitated the removal of a parish church of that name. It was probably here that the shrine of St Erkenwald stood until it was moved to the area of the High Altar in 1148. It was also here that the Fraternity of the Holy Name (also known as the Fraternity of Jesus) met during the Middle Ages. St Faith's Chapel continued to serve the parish of the same name until 1551 and was also the church of the Company of Stationers, which still sometimes meets here.

To its east stands the OBE Chapel, where members of the Order of the British Empire come to worship, to be married, and to have their children baptised. The Order was established by King George V in 1917 in recognition of the role played by women in World War I. Its glass screens are etched with images of George VI and Queen Elizabeth, Queen Elizabeth II and Prince Philip, and with motifs celebrating the Commonwealth including kangaroos and Canadian 'Mounties'. In the ceiling is set a golden shell, the symbol of St James and of pilgrims. To the south-east is a chapel recently dedicated for the use of the Imperial Society of Knights Bachelor, which offers a place of quiet prayer for all in a busy cathedral.

4

5

6

9

10

7

8

5 Humming bird by Haslop from the American Memorial Chapel.
6 Virgin and Child by Josefina de Vasconcellos, the crypt. 7 Dove, symbolising the Holy Spirit, in stained glass in the American Memorial Chapel.
8 American eagle in the American Memorial Chapel.
9 Stained glass depicting Noah's Ark from the American Memorial Chapel.
10 *The Light of the World* by William Holman Hunt, in the Middlesex Chapel, north transept.

6

A resting place: the crypt

The timeless, grounded atmosphere of the crypt is the Cathedral's foremost burial place, where many of those who have made an outstanding contribution to the life of the nation and of the world now rest. One of the earliest of these was St Erkenwald, who may have been buried beneath the stone church he erected here in 685 until his relics were moved to the High Altar in 1148. St Faith's Chapel, beneath the quire, may mark its site. Many monuments can be seen in the crypt, where the well-regarded were buried in its earthen floor. This is now paved with stone, tile and mosaics; the mosaics recall the ancient Roman origins of the site, and some of them were laid by women prisoners from Woking Gaol during the nineteenth century, when the crypt was opened for viewing.

The national heroes whose tombs now dominate the crypt are Horatio, Lord Nelson, who died in the midst of his great victory at the Battle of Trafalgar in 1805, and the Duke of Wellington, who won another great battle against Napoleonic forces at Waterloo in Belgium in 1815. After his victory Wellington wrote, 'Nothing except a battle lost can be half so melancholy as a battle won.' His imposing state funeral, his coffin borne upon a splendid carriage, took place here in 1852, and the banners used then surround his tomb. Nelson's tomb stands in the atmospherically lit central vaulted chamber beneath the dome, in the place where his coffin was lowered from the Cathedral above during his state funeral. The elegant black casket on top was designed to receive the mortal remains of Cardinal Wolsey, but he fell from King Henry VIII's favour during the Reformation and was denied a grand burial. It remained at Windsor Castle, in St George's Chapel, until a suitable recipient was found, and the cardinal's hat was replaced with Nelson's viscount's coronet.

East of this is another chamber containing a simple, massive sarcophagus of Cornish granite, watched over by four guardian lions. Herein lies Wellington.

In addition to such leaders, the ordinary people whose lives have been caught up in the maelstrom of conflicts beyond their control are remembered in many of the memorials here: soldiers, sailors, airmen, war correspondents, nurses, local guides and auxiliaries and many more – from many nations. Prison reformers, politicians, campaigners for nuclear disarmament, scholars, scientists, musicians, artists and architects are all remembered. They include Florence Nightingale (depicted by A. G. Walker), the heroine of the Crimea who did so much to establish the nursing profession; Lawrence of Arabia; the Elizabethan warrior-poet Philip Sidney; George Washington – first President of the USA; John Wycliffe, who translated the Bible into English and was condemned as a heretic for his pains; Sir William Howard Russell – the first war correspondent who reported the Crimean War; Alexander Fleming, who invented penicillin; Henry Wellcome, who founded the Wellcome Institute for the History and Understanding of Medicine and the Wellcome Foundation; the composer and music publisher Ivor Novello; Arthur Sullivan

Bronze Crucifixion by John Singer Sargent, gracing the artist's monument in the crypt.

1

2

3

4

5

of Gilbert and Sullivan fame; architect Edwin Lutyens; the artists Joshua Reynolds, Anthony Van Dyck, Joseph William Mallard Turner, John Constable, William Holman Hunt, John Everett Millais, William Blake, Lord Leighton, Edwin Landseer, caricaturist Max Beerbohm and Randolph Caldecott – illustrator of children's books, whose image appears on a medallion held by a child on his monument designed by Alfred Gilbert.

Sir Christopher Wren is himself interred in the south-east aisle of the crypt, his grave marked by a simple stone slab. On the wall above is a further memorial tablet set up by his son, Christopher (who wrote a biography of Wren entitled *Parentalia*), which carries the epitaph: 'Beneath lies buried the founder of this church and city, Christopher Wren, who lived more than 90 years, not for himself but for the public good. Reader, if you seek his monument, look around you.' Another plaque recalls the craftspeople who helped Wren to realise his vision. On the adjacent window sill sits a block of Portland stone, from which the Cathedral is constructed, bearing on one end Wren's own mason's mark, indicating that he selected this chunk of masonry as worthy for inclusion whilst visiting a quarry in Dorset on the south-west coast of England.

Other memorials record the lives of many people who are less famous but also made a great difference to their societies or were the victims of conflicts: the Boer War, Gallipoli, Korea, the South Atlantic and the Gulf wars. There are memorials to Professor Gordon Hamilton-Fairley, killed by a terrorist bomb in 1975, whose epitaph reads: 'It matters not how a man dies but how he lives', and Robert Douglas Eaton, a former chorister of St Paul's who lost his life when the World Trade Centre was destroyed by a cataclysmic act of terrorism on 11 September 2001.

Some of the tombs from the pre-fire cathedral, damaged as they came crashing down from the Cathedral above, can still be seen in the crypt aisles. Burials inside church buildings are now prohibited on public health grounds, but memorials are still sometimes erected today. A recent addition to the crypt is the imposing screen by metalworker James Horrobin, installed in 2004 to commemorate Sir Winston Churchill, who led Britain as its Prime Minister during World War II and whose state funeral took place at St Paul's in 1965. Other notable works include the bronze monuments to Lord Leighton by Sir Thomas Brock, Auguste Rodin's bust of the poet W. E. Henley, and the bronze cast of John Singer Sargent's *Crucifixion* on his own monument. There is also a dignified sculpture of the Virgin and Child by Josefina de Vasconcellos.

Within the crypt the living also find rest, in quiet reflection in one of the chapels. Other parts of the crypt are more lively. In the exhibition gallery (with metal gates by Alan Evans) visitors can find out more about the Cathedral, with the help of video and IT resources, and can explore its treasures (including plate on loan from other London churches, much of St Paul's own plate having been stolen in 1810) and its story. There is an education centre where school groups are welcomed, the conference centre where many stimulating debates and events are held, and the shop, cafés and other services that help visitors to enjoy their time here.

Monuments in the crypt include: 1 South Africa campaign, 1899–1902. 2 Ivor Novello. 3 A pre-fire tomb effigy. 4 Gallipoli landings, 1915–16. 5 Bust of T. E. Lawrence (Lawrence of Arabia) by Eric Kennington. 6 Nelson mosaic. 7 The casket from the Nelson Chamber. 8 Memorial to the South Atlantic Task Force (1982). 9 Memorial to the Pre-Raphaelite artist Millais. 10 Memorial to the artist William Turner. 11 The OBE Chapel kneelers and altar frontal. 12 Memorial to the artist William Blake. 13 A Sikh guards the memorial to General Sir Samuel James Browne of the Indian Army. 14 Granite lion supporting the tomb of the Duke of Wellington. 15 Wren's tomb. 16 Memorial to the scientists Alexander Fleming, Henry Wellcome and Professor Gordon Hamilton-Fairley. 17 Grave of the composer Arthur Sullivan. 18 Monument to the nurse Florence Nightingale. 19 Monument to the illustrator Randolph Caldecott. 20 Admiral Nelson's tomb in the Nelson Chamber. 21 Monument to George Frampton, sculptor. 22 Memorial to those killed during an expedition to the Sinai Desert in 1882, led by Professor Henry Palmer and including his Syrian and Hebrew helpers.

6

7

8

9

10

11

12

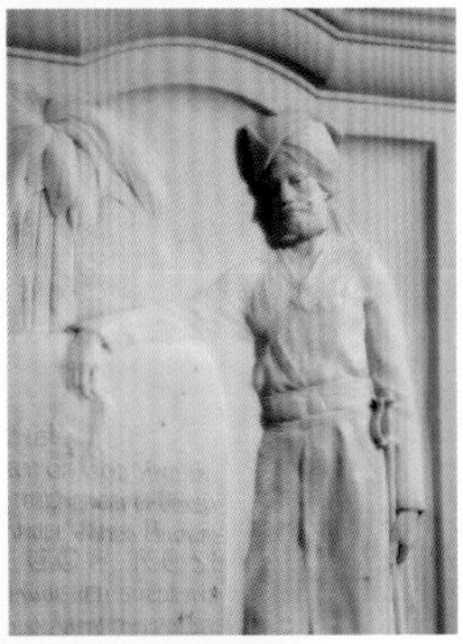

13

14

15

16

17–19

20

21

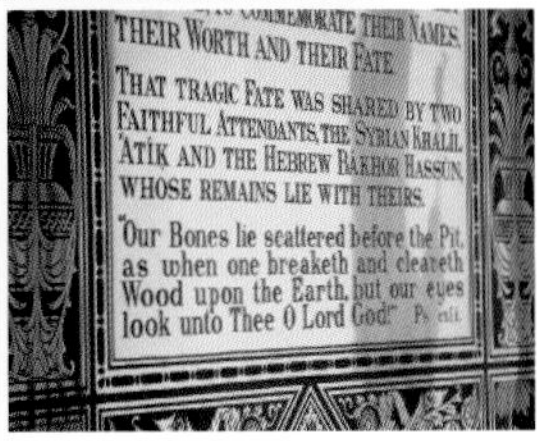

22

7

The secret cathedral

The secret life of public buildings can be fascinating. Behind the scenes lurk warrens of hidden rooms and spaces where the everyday business of running and caring for such buildings takes place. Even in the Anglo-Saxon period, when the Cathedral was founded, large churches would sometimes have two storeys and would have rooms in their towers where people worked, meetings would be held, manuscripts penned and things not in use would be stored. This is still pretty much the case today. The following introduces some of the more formal areas that can be visited, some by special tour, behind the scenes at St Paul's.

The Galleries

Inside the dome, up 259 steps, is the Whispering Gallery where it is said that a whisper against the wall on one side can be heard 32 metres away on the other. From here there are marvellous views of the Cathedral floor, the Thornhill paintings and the dome mosaics.

On the outside of the dome, up 378 steps, is the Stone Gallery, and above this, just below the lantern and up 570 steps, is the Golden Gallery. Both offer stunning 360-degree views of London. Visitors have been climbing the steps to marvel at these views of the interior and exterior of St Paul's for over 300 years – just as their forebears climbed its spectacular medieval spire.

The Geometric Staircase and the Towers

At the base of the north-west tower is the chapel of All Souls (see page 58). In the south-west tower ascends the geometric staircase, or Dean's staircase, a marvel of engineering and architectural design built by William Kempster. The stairs appear to float, unsupported, their stone treads cantilevered out from the wall, with each step supporting the next. This is almost a state staircase and must have been intended to allow not only the Dean and Chapter but also VIP visitors (including monarchs) access to the triforium level to view the library and trophy room and to take in the sweeping views of the nave from the western gallery. From here the external gallery of the upper peristyle of the west façade could be accessed. Here Wren placed a stone pulpit.

In the north-west tower is the bellringers' chamber where the twelve bells that sound the peal are rung. They commemorate Baroness Burdett-Coutts, 'Queen of the Poor', who championed public housing during the nineteenth century. In the south-west tower hangs Great Tom, the largest swinging bell in Europe, presented in 1716, which strikes the hour and tolls at the death of royalty and senior clergy, and also Great Paul (or the Recall Bell, because it called the London apprentices back to work after lunch), which strikes at 1.00pm each day.

The geometric (or Dean's) staircase, looking upwards into the south-west tower, with balustrades by Tijou.

1

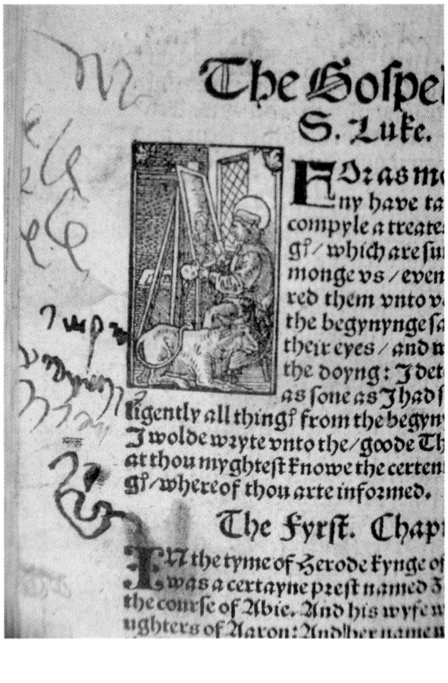

2

1 Statues of cathedral worthies, the south triforium. 2 Opening of St Luke's Gospel, with marginal pen-trials, from Tyndale's *New Testament* printed in English in Worms, 1526. Facing page The Library, south triforium.

Also in the south-west tower is the great clock with three faces, by John Smith and Sons of Derby, added in 1893. It has been suggested that Wren once considered housing an enormous telescope in this tower, which would have formed an observatory.

The Triforium

This is the gallery that runs midway around the interior of the Cathedral beneath the upper clerestory windows and above the aisles. It is named for the 'three parts' of the nave, its aisles, and the gallery above. It is quite wide and was designed to provide a useful series of areas where various functions associated with the running of the Cathedral could take place.

In the north triforium is the Trophy Room (see page 71), outside of which are exhibited a wooden pulpit by Robert Mylne (1802) and the Italian marble pulpit designed by F. C. Penrose in 1888–1891 to accompany Bodley and Garner's altar and reredos. Large plans and drawings of the Cathedral, by surveyors such as Cecil Brown, are also displayed here.

In the south triforium, at its western end, is the library (see below). The long room next to this has been used to store items from the Cathedral collections and stones from the earlier cathedrals that have been found during excavations. It is hoped that this may become a more formal exhibition gallery, but the layout of the Cathedral and its sensitivity as an important listed building means that only limited public access to the triforium is possible, as part of special guided tours.

The Library

Books and documents would have featured in the life of St Paul's and the liturgy since its very beginnings. St Mellitus would have come equipped with books, some from Gregory the Great's Rome. Literacy was introduced and the scribes of St Paul's would have written books and charters from the seventh century onwards. Medieval book lists from the Cathedral, the earliest dating from the thirteenth century, include references to an ancient psalter owned by St Erkenwald and to another, glossed between the lines in Old English. A cathedral dignitary, the Master of the Schools (the first of whom, Master Durand, was a canon by 1086), served as the librarian, a post that later passed to the Treasurer. Some special copies of sacred texts were also kept at the High Altar, or in cupboards beside it, during the Middle Ages. Archives were also kept, in the Treasury, although the pre-Conquest charters seem to have been largely destroyed, necessitating a campaign of forgeries during the early twelfth century. Cartularies were compiled from the mid-twelfth century onwards, including the *Liber Pilosus* or 'hairy book' (compiled in 1241–2), so called because of its binding.

Authors and other members of the cathedral clergy would also have given books to the library, including the chronicler Ralph de Diceto who began a survey of the estates when appointed dean in 1180. The role of the Cathedral as a centre of legal studies would also have occasioned the production and acquisition of books. In the 1440s Prebendary Walter Sherrington established a chantry chapel and a new library, the latter situated over the east wing of the Pardon Churchyard cloister.

1

By the Reformation the Cathedral possessed a fine library and the well-ordered archives of the bishopric, Dean and Chapter, and the College of Minor Canons. Alas, most of these were lost or alienated during the Great Fire of London in 1666, although many books and archives were evacuated to Fulham, Islington and Sion College. Other books left the library during the century before the fire, with some finding their way to the collections of Archbishop Matthew Parker (including Corpus Christi College Library, MS 383, an important early Anglo-Saxon collection of laws) and to the heirs of Sir Robert Cotton (including the base of a dish converted into a medieval tonsure-plate – now in the British Museum – used when shaving the heads of priests). The greatest number of surviving St Paul's manuscripts are now in Aberdeen University Library, presented by a friend of Patrick Young, who had been the royal librarian and a prebendary of St Paul's (1621–1652).

2

Only a shelf-full of manuscripts and early printed books now survives in the Cathedral Library, but these include a twelfth-century illuminated psalter, a fourteenth-century illuminated copy of the *Canon of Medicine*, and contemporary handwritten copies of the poems and sermons of the early seventeenth-century poet-Dean John Donne. Attempts to restock the library after the fire involved the purchase of the library of the late Robert Grey, former vicar of Islington, and a valuable collection of biblical editions belonging to Humphrey Wanley, librarian of the Harley Collection of the Earls of Oxford, which included one of the world's three surviving copies of Tyndale's *New Testament*, printed in English in Worms in 1526 for export to England. For this Tyndale was condemned for heresy, but it helped place the Gospel into the hands of ordinary people, who previously had largely relied for their biblical knowledge on preaching, readings during church services, prayers, tracts and images.

Wren planned two libraries within the new Cathedral, in the north and south triforium aisles at the east end of the building. That on the south is approached by the grand geometric staircase and was fitted out as a library in 1708–9. It remains largely unaltered today, apart from its heating and lighting. Its wooden floor, shelving and balustraded gallery were made under the supervision of Sir Charles Hopson, Wren's master joiner from 1706–9. Its ornate cantilevered brackets were carved by Jonathan Maine in 1709. The stone pilasters, with their trophies – in ancient Roman fashion – of floral garlands, books, scrolls, inkwells, quill pens and skulls (a *memento mori* or reminder of mortality), were skilfully carved by a team led by master mason William Kempster, who also worked on the south-west tower.

This is the working library of Dean and Chapter. It consists mostly of works written by them and books on theology, the Cathedral, its history and music, sermons and tracts. It also contains a number of artefacts such as busts of cathedral worthies and portraits, including that of Bishop Compton, which hangs above the fireplace. Amongst those who most concerned themselves with the library in recent times were Canons Sydney Smith, William Hale Hale and John Collins. They were

3

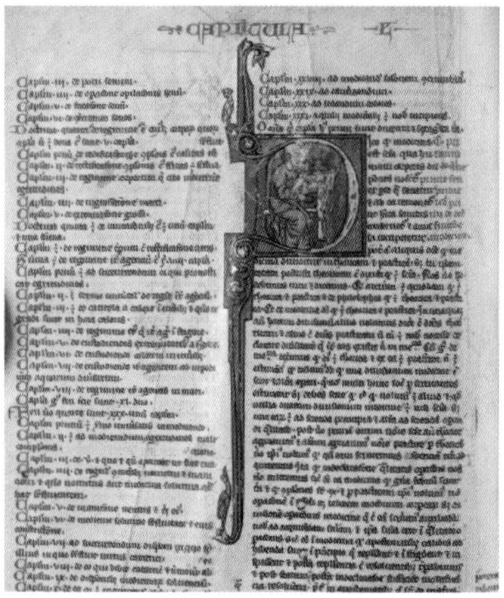

4

1–2 The Library, south triforium.
3 Detail from twelfth-century psalter: the saints noted for devotion within it indicate that it may have been made for St Paul's use.
4 The famous Islamic scholar Avicenna, seated at his desk, from a fourteenth-century copy of the *Canon of Medicine*, presented to the Cathedral Library in 1451 by Dr John Somerset, physician to King Henry IV.

ably assisted by the cathedral librarians, notable amongst whom was W. Sparrow Simpson, librarian from 1861–1897, who did much to research and catalogue the collections and build up its music holdings. The library now houses around 30,000 items. Most of the archives of Dean and Chapter and of the Minor Canons have been housed at the Guildhall Library since 1980, these include drawings from Wren's office, others are at All Souls College, Oxford.

In 2004 the ongoing work of cataloguing the collections resulted in an inventory, in which most of them are described. The Cathedral retains a large architectural archive of drawings, plans and photographs relating to the fabric and to works undertaken from the nineteenth century onwards. Over the door of the librarian's office is inscribed: 'Of making many books there is no end'. Sure enough, new books and archival materials, on paper and computer screen, are added to the collections daily. Likewise, the commitment of the current Dean and Chapter to enhancing the art holdings with contemporary works allows the Cathedral's collections to continue to grow in the present generation.

The Trophy Room

The library that Wren planned for the north triforium was not fitted out as such, and became known as the Trophy Room when the naval trophies of Nelson's victory at Trafalgar were displayed there following his death during the battle in 1805 and his subsequent burial at St Paul's.

It originally contained Wren's Great Model, commissioned by King Charles II in 1674 (and made by the Cleeres at a cost of £600 – the price of a good London house) to support his second design, which was rejected in 1673. The model is made of oak and plaster and is constructed to a scale of 1.24 inches (3.8cm) to the foot (30.5cm), being 13ft (3.95m) high and 13ft 1in (3.97m) long. To satisfy the clergy, this design had a nave, but retained a resplendent dome. The prospective patrons were even able to enter the model to view the interior, like Alice in Wonderland. It was rejected due to its resemblance to St Peter's in Rome and the Sorbonne in Paris, and its heroic style, redolent of the theatrical Baroque architecture of the Catholic Counter-Reformation.

The Great Model now once again occupies the Trophy Room and forms the centrepiece of a display charting the evolution of Wren's vision for the new cathedral.

5

6

7

5 Stair to the organ loft. 6–7 Wren's Great Model, the Trophy Room, north triforium.

Cathedral City

1

2

3

1 Above the saucer domes.
2 The choristers rehearsing. 3 *The Old Deanery*, by John Crowther, 1881.
Facing page The dome, seen through a grille from the crypt.

The Chapter House, where the Dean and Chapter meet to discuss cathedral business, was sited in the south churchyard, in the south-west angle of the transept, during the Middle Ages. Wren built a new chapter house to the north of the Cathedral. This was destroyed during the Blitz and after the war the then Surveyor to the Fabric, Godfrey Allen, constructed the current red-brick building to resemble it. The Cathedral's administrative staff now work here, and there are large and small chapter rooms where the Dean and Chapter meet regularly and entertain guests.

The busy works department is situated beneath the Cathedral precincts and undertakes the ongoing work of maintaining and preserving this building of national and international heritage value. A workforce of electricians, joiners, plumbers and other tradespeople are forever caring for the Cathedral under the supervision of the Clerk of Works. The conservation, renovation and any new designs relating to the building and its estate are all overseen by a leading conservation architect, known as the Surveyor to the Fabric. Those who have held this post are commemorated by a memorial in the crypt.

Those caring for the collections, including the Cathedral Librarian, the Architectural Archivist, the Conservator and those who help them on specific projects or as volunteers, work at the triforium level, in the warren of offices and spaces provided by Wren.

Some other members of cathedral staff are based in Amen Court, the current equivalent of the traditional cathedral close, off nearby Ave Maria Lane. The Dean and residentiary members of Chapter, the Minor Canons, the Registrar and some of the musicians also have homes here. The three houses forming Amen Court were supplemented with a complex of buildings, in Jacobean style, constructed in 1878–1880 by Ewan Christian. The three elegant houses originally built in 1671–3 under Edward Woodroffe still survive on its south side. In the basement of one of these is the St Paul's Institute – an exciting new initiative designed to promote awareness and discussion of the ethical issues surrounding business and commerce in the world today.

Just to the east of the Cathedral stands the Cathedral School, incorporating the tower of St Augustine's Church, on the ancient Roman road of Watling Street, which was decommissioned after severe bomb damage in the Blitz. The choir school opened on this new site on 4 May 1967 and in 1997 the word 'choir' was dropped from its title to reflect its broader composition and educational aims. Children between the ages of four and thirteen, boys and girls, are educated here – including the Cathedral's choristers, whose education is largely funded by the Dean and Chapter and who can spend up to 22 hours per week singing at cathedral services and concerts.

8 The **cathedral** in context

From as early as 704 the Cathedral precinct was known as *Paulesbyrig* – a special enclosure within the City of London. The degree of public access to this precinct fluctuated over the ages and was sometimes a source of friction between the occupants of Cathedral and City. Its medieval parameters were defined by its ranges of buildings and sometimes by walls and gates. Wren disliked the railings placed around his building but those that still survive on the north side are greatly valued today. Temple Bar was re-sited next to the Chapter House in 2004, recalling these earlier gates. It was designed by Wren and erected in Fleet Street by the Inns of Court known as The Temple. In modern times it became an obstruction to motor vehicles and was moved to the grounds of Theobald's Park, Hertfordshire, where it gradually fell into disrepair until the Corporation of London decided to restore and reconstruct it as part of the Paternoster development.

Wren's imposing portico was built with two levels – the Great Model only has one, but massive enough stones could not be found. It is surmounted by Bird's carving on the pediment depicting the conversion of St Paul and is crowned by his statues of Saints Paul, Peter and James. The north transept portico was inspired by that of Santa Maria della Pace in Rome, which Wren never visited but which he admired from prints. The south transept portico is surmounted by a sculpture of a phoenix rising triumphant, like the Cathedral, from the ashes. In front of the west façade stands a statue of Queen Anne, in whose reign Wren's building was completed. Bird's original statue decayed and was replaced in 1885. She faces towards Ludgate Hill, occasioning the early eighteenth-century ballad:

> Brandy Nan, Brandy Nan,
> They've left you in the lurch,
> Facing towards the gin shops,
> With your back towards the church.

People have been buried at St Paul's since its foundation (some burials dating from the fourth, eighth and ninth centuries have been excavated on its northern side). The clergy had their own cemetery in the precincts and the plot dedicated to lay people was to the north and east of the Cathedral building. So many were buried there over the ages that disturbed bones were gathered up into a charnel house. The great and the good were buried here (or in very special circumstances within the Cathedral itself) and included the parents of Thomas Becket, near to whom many burghers wished to be interred; but the destitute also found a resting place here. The north churchyard became known as the 'Pardon Churchyard', perhaps due to its use during the Black Death of 1348–9. To acknowledge that all were equal in death, a set of painted panels depicting the Dance of Death was commissioned by John Carpenter around 1430, perhaps to

The north transept portal, with surrounding shops, giving an impression of the earlier street plan.

YOUNG'S
glo
orange

1

2

1 The Cathedral and the Millennium Bridge. 2 Plaque marking the site of St Paul's Cross, an ancient place of public assembly and debate, north churchyard. 3 Wren's Temple Bar. 4 *A Windy Day in St Paul's Churchyard* by Robert Dighton, eighteenth century, showing the window of Bowles the printmaker, one of many purveyors of word and image that clustered around the Cathedral. Facing page North West tower with the Swiss-Re building behind (affectionately known as the 'gherkin').

3

commemorate the famous mayor, Richard (Dick) Whittington. They were hung in the cloister within the Pardon Churchyard, featuring images and verses in English composed by John Lydgate, and became a tourist sight known as the 'dance of Pauls'.

Today a column surmounted by a gilded statue of St Paul, commemorating Paul's Cross, presides over the north churchyard. This north-east corner was once the assembly place of the *folkmoot*, a democratic gathering of the people to determine their affairs and government that originated in the Anglo-Saxon period. Just to the north of the east end of the Cathedral is an inscription, set in the ground, commemorating the actual site of Paul's Cross, the Cathedral's external pulpit and a place where news and views were for centuries proclaimed – a monument to the origins of free speech. It is joined by a memorial carved by Richard Kindersley, set in the ground before the north transept steps, commemorating the 40,000 or more people who lost their lives in London during the Blitz, when the environs of St Paul's were largely flattened. Near by stands a statue of John Wesley, founder of Methodism, who regularly worshipped there in the eighteenth century.

In the south churchyard stood the medieval vaulted chapter house. Its foundations have recently been excavated and will form the basis of a new landscaping scheme for the churchyard in which a scaled-down depiction of the ground plan of the great medieval cathedral will also be set. The image of the Annunciation above the south door meant that this area was also a popular place of pilgrimage and gathering before the Reformation.

Paternoster Row, which runs beside the north churchyard, became a radical intellectual and publishing hub from the Middle Ages onwards. The warren of medieval streets is still echoed by the passageways between the modern office buildings and shops there. The area was flattened during the Blitz and redeveloped in unsympathetic fashion during the 1960s. It has recently been redeveloped again, in the conservative neo-classical style advocated by Prince Charles. A great gilded flame-topped column now stands at the heart of Paternoster Square, where workers and tourists gather on warm summer days. With only a little imagination it is possible to people it with the bustle of thinkers, communicators and craftspeople who have helped to shape our history.

St Paul's dome is complemented in the City townscape by the delicate spires and towers of Wren's city churches – 53 of them originally – which he designed as part of his projected planning of the post-fire City. These include St Mary le Bow, St Bride's and St Stephen Walbrook. Along with the Cathedral these churches offer a place of spiritual refreshment and quiet sanctuary for the City's workers. Each year, as part of the City of London Festival, a lively series of musical events and arts installations are held in them – and in the Cathedral, the mother church around which they cluster.

4

9

Epilogue

That's where we've been – this is where we're going

Even now, when the modern buildings of the City tower ever higher, the great dome of St Paul's still forms a prominent landmark on the skyline – a potent symbol reminding us of our past, and a source of inspiration for our future.

Led by the Dean and Chapter, along with the Registrar, a committed and varied group of people care for St Paul's and those who visit and worship there. It stands at the heart of the vibrant diocese of London, under the pastoral care of the Bishop of London, whose clergy and parishioners often attend services and events.

The liturgical round of services takes place each day, offering up worship and praise. In a diverse and vibrant city such as London, St Paul's is a public, sacred space offering people from any background or belief the opportunity to hear the ancient wisdom of Scripture and the beauty of music, and to see the majesty of a building that was itself built as a prayer, reaching for the reality of God beyond us. People come to share in the worship and to pray in its chapels, City workers and visitors find it a place of spiritual refreshment, and tourists, schoolchildren and educational groups are stimulated by one of Britain's most beautiful buildings and leading heritage sites. Major services and affairs of state see packed congregations – in 2005 these have included services of remembrance for the victims of the South Asian tsunami and the London bombings; the celebration of the founding of the United Nations and the commemoration of the Battle of Trafalgar and death of Nelson. The Cathedral is also filled with people during the many concerts and lectures held in the course of a year. More experimental acts of worship are also held regularly at St Paul's featuring key speakers, popular, folk, and world music and liturgical dance.

The cleaning and restoration of the interior and exterior is nearing completion, conducted by a skilled workforce under the dedicated supervision of Surveyor to the Fabric Martin Stancliffe and Clerk of Works Martin Fletcher. Already the breathtaking splendour of Wren's original vision and the contributions of successive generations to the fabric and decoration have become more apparent and better understood. The programme of works also offers opportunities for archaeological excavations, conducted by the Cathedral Archaeologist who is based at the nearby Museum of London, which are giving valuable insights into the previous cathedral buildings and precincts and the city in which they functioned. A massive, award-winning study of the history of St Paul's was published in 2004 to celebrate its 1,400th anniversary, edited by Derek Keene, Arthur Burns and Andrew Saint, with contributions by many gifted scholars. Contemporary artworks are being displayed and commissioned, with the generous aid of donors. The Cathedral collections are being conserved under the supervision of the Cathedral Conservator and made more accessible, and the story of this remarkable place is being more fully interpreted and opened up to a wide-ranging local, national and international audience.

An exciting recent initiative is the St Paul's Institute, which was established in 2002 to promote debate and action on the ethical issues surrounding business, globalisation, poverty and the environment. It has organised the St Paul's Ethics Lectures, featuring Nobel Prize winners; 'The Worlds We Live In', a series of dialogues between the Archbishop of Canterbury and international experts on politics, economics, the environment and public health; and the programme 'Global Poverty: What Can One Person Do?' In 2005 a massive 'Make Poverty History' white band was wrapped around the dome, signalling support for the ongoing campaign for a fairer world and reduction of global poverty and needless suffering. Sir Bob Geldof and Kofi Annan are amongst those who have addressed capacity audiences on these subjects in recent years at the Institute.

The pastoral work of St Paul's embraces not only those who enter through its doors, with members of the clergy always ready to listen to those who need them; but in the desire to bear witness to God's love in the world it extends far beyond.

The Cathedral can seldom have felt so warm and welcoming. Yet, sadly, an admission charge currently has to be made, as has so often been the case in the past, for although St Paul's is primarily a place of worship and is always freely open to all for services and private prayer in a dedicated chapel, it is also a major heritage site and visitor attraction, requiring large and continuous injections of cash for its upkeep. Funding is not available from the central Church authorities or from the state and has to be raised largely from tourist revenue (which can be precarious and unpredictable), grant bodies and individual and corporate donations. Grappling with the realities of life and finances at the heart of a leading centre of commerce has always been a challenge for those who care for St Paul's, for their agendas are not solely those of the world. They seek to reach out and embrace it, as a visible beacon of God's love for Creation, and to transcend it, helping the human spirit to soar towards that love. This is what St Paul's is all about.

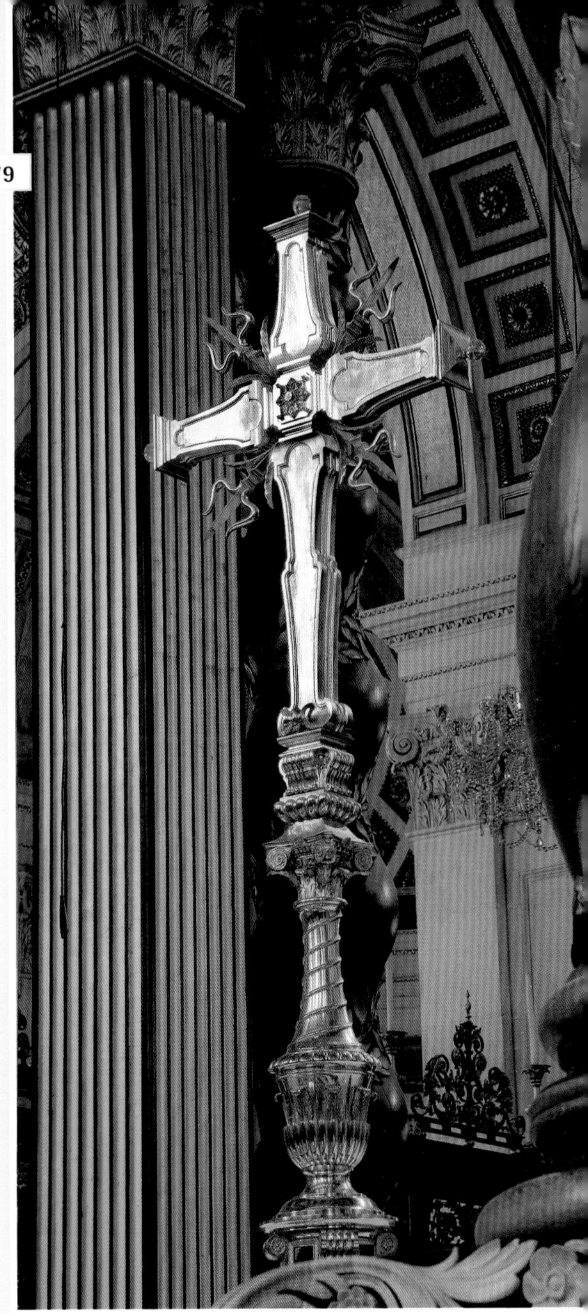
1

2

3

4

5

6

1 High Altar cross. 2 Kofi Annan debates the UN Millennium Campaign. 3 Sankta Lucia carol service. 4 Advent carol service. 5 St Paul's Institute debate. 6 Choristers.

Visitor Information

St Paul's Cathedral needs your help

You can help us enormously to maintain the fabric of this beautiful Wren Cathedral, with its renowned musical traditions and fine collections, not only by your visits and purchases in the shop and catering facilities but through membership of the Friends of St Paul's, a Gift-Aided donation or a gift in your Will towards the Cathedral or an aspect of its work. Please contact the Foundation Office, The Chapter House, St Paul's Churchyard, London EC4M 8AD. Telephone (020) 7246 8371 or visit www.stpaulscathedral.org.uk for further information.

First published in 2006 by Jarrold Publishing, Whitefriars, Norwich NR3 1JR
Telephone 01603 677318
www.jarrold-publishing.co.uk

All rights reserved. No part of this publication may be reproduced, stored in a retrieval system, or transmitted, in any form or by any means, without the prior permission of the publisher and any other copyright holders.

© St Paul's Cathedral and Jarrold Publishing

Text by Professor Michelle P. Brown
© St Paul's Cathedral

All photographs in this book were taken by Peter Smith of Newbery Smith Photography and are © Jarrold Publishing, with the exception of: Philip Way p31 (6, 7, 8), p79 (2, 3, 4, 5); Malcolm Crampton p29 (5); AF Kersting p12 (1); Sampson Lloyd p17 (4), p19 (3), p20 (2), p22 (1, 3, 4, 5), p26 (2, 3), p28 (3), p32 (2), p48 (1); Bridgeman Art Library p20 (1, 3), p21, p24 (3), p26 (1, 2), p72 (3); Jarrold Publishing p20 (2); Getty Images p31 (5); Guildhall Library p14 (4), p24 (4); Mercers' Company Archives & Art Collection p16 (2); Society of Antiquaries p18 (1, 2); Museum of London p12 (2); British Library p14 (1), p15 (3); St Paul's Cathedral Library p13 (3), p14 (1), p16 (1), p24 (2), p30 (1, 2, 3, 4), p44 (1), p68 (2), p70 (3, 4), p76 (4)

Designed and produced by Jarrold Publishing

Designer: Kaarin Wall
Editor: Sally Whitman
Repro: Kevin Parker and Martin Kempson
Creative Director: Malcolm Crampton

ISBN-13: 978-0-7117-4222-2
ISBN-10: 0-7117-4222-7
Printed in Great Britain 40550-1/06

Visitor Information

Services take place on weekdays and Saturdays at 7.30am (Mattins), 8.00am (Holy Communion), 12.30pm (Holy Communion) and 5.00pm (Choral Evensong). The timing occasionally varies for special services. A chapel is available for private prayer. Sunday worship is at 8.00am (Holy Communion), 10.15am (Choral Mattins with sermon), 11.30am (Choral Eucharist with sermon, 11am in July), 3.15pm (Choral Evensong with sermon), 6.00pm (Evening Service).

The Cathedral is open to visitors at the following times, from Monday to Saturday. The Cathedral, crypt and ambulatory open at 8.30am. The Whispering Gallery, Stone Gallery and Golden Gallery open at 9.30am. Last admission to all parts of the Cathedral is at 4.00pm. Special services or events may close all or part of the Cathedral at short notice.

Cafés, toilets and the Cathedral Shop are located in the crypt. Mobile phones should be turned off and photography is not permitted inside the Cathedral.

If you are interested in joining the Friends of St Paul's, supporting its work and enjoying its benefits, please write to The Secretary, The Friends of St Paul's, Chapter House, St Paul's Churchyard, London EC4M 8AD.

Information concerning the Cathedral, its collections, services, sermons, events, concerts and the programme of the St Paul's Institute can be found at:

www.stpauls.co.uk
Telephone (020) 7246 8348

For information on the Cathedral Shop, visit www.stpaulsshop.co.uk

Author's acknowledgements

I should like to take this opportunity to thank the following: the Bishop of London, the Rt Revd and Rt Hon (Dr) Richard Chartres; the Dean of St Paul's, the Very Revd Dr John Moses and my Chapter colleagues; the Minor Canons; the Registrar, Major General John Milne; the Surveyor to the Fabric, Martin Stancliffe; the Cathedral Librarian, Joseph Wisdom; Architectural Archivist Christine Faunch; Cathedral Conservator Teresa Heady; Cathedral Archaeologist John Schofield; the Virgers; the Education and Stewards Departments; the Working Friends; the St Paul's Institute and St Paul's Foundation; members of the Fabric Advisory Committee; and many other colleagues amongst the staff and volunteers who care for St Paul's. I should especially like to thank Peter Smith for his stunning new photography and Philip Way for his images of people and events at the Cathedral; Mark McVay, the Cathedral's Director of Marketing, and Malcolm Crampton of Jarrold Publishing for their invaluable support, enthusiasm and collaboration on this project – and also my dear husband, Cecil Brown.

Further reading

Sir William Dugdale, *The History of St Paul's Cathedral in London* (1658)
Christopher Wren, *Parentalia, or, Memoirs of the Family of the Wrens* (1750)
Dean H. H. Milman, *Annals of S. Paul's* (1868)
G. L. Prestige, *St Paul's in its Glory, 1831–1911* (1955)
J. Lang, *Rebuilding St Paul's after the Great Fire of London* (1956)
Dean W. Matthews and W. M. Atkins, eds, *History of St Paul's* (1957)
K. Downes, *The Architecture of Wren* (1982, reptd 1988)
F. Atkinson, *St Paul's and the City* (1985)
P. Burman, *St Paul's Cathedral* (1987)
A. Saunders, *St Paul's, The Story of the Cathedral* (2001)
D. Keene, A. Burns and A. Saint, eds, *St Paul's, the Cathedral Church of London, 604–2004* (2004)